Ghosts of Clinton County

Ghosts

of Clinton County

Gordie Little

North Country Books, Inc.

Utica, New York

Ghosts of Clinton County
Copyright © 2009
by Gordie Little

ISBN-10 1-59531-031-2
ISBN-13 978-1-59531-031-6

Design by Zach Steffen & Rob Igoe, Jr.

Library of Congress Cataloging-in-Publication Data

Little, Gordie.
Ghosts of Clinton County / Gordie Little.
p. cm.
Includes bibliographical references and index.
ISBN 978-1-59531-031-6 (alk. paper)
1. Ghosts--New York--Clinton County. I. Title.
BF1472.U6L58 2009
133.109747'54--dc22

                              2009029210

North Country Books, Inc.
220 Lafayette Street
Utica, New York 13502
www.northcountrybooks.com

Contents

Preface

Growing up as a "preacher's kid," I always believed that the spirit survives life on earth as we know it. I have a passionate interest in anything that approaches the supernatural. Since the 1960s I have conducted numerous informal ESP experiments using a variety of methods.

After finishing a three-and-a-half decade radio career in 1997, I began seriously collecting, writing, and telling "true" ghost stories. Some are heartwarming and others are spine-tingling.

Almost everyone with whom I speak has had one or more experiences that seem to defy explanation. Each time I present my stories in public, members of the audience gather round to tell me theirs. My collection has grown almost exponentially. It's time to share it with a wider audience by putting a select group of these stories in print.

Ghosts in Our House

This is a true story about ongoing supernatural activity in the old Morrisonville, New York, home that our family has occupied since the early 1970s. Many of the observations are my own. Others were related to me by relatives or by individuals who lived in the house before us.

Early deeds tell us the structure was built in the 1880s but wasn't a dwelling until much later. It actually started out as a barn or outbuilding and was part of an estate belonging to Frank Rugar, a prominent local businessman in the late nineteenth and early twentieth centuries. The original portion was used to store tools and machinery and perhaps house horses. Later owners, Jim and Jane Olsen, turned it into a small, two-story home. Just after 1950, a large addition was attached, and the house was ultimately expanded to include six bedrooms.

On April 30, 1956, Vincent Olsen, the four-year-old son of Jim and Jane, was tragically drowned in the raging spring flow of the Saranac River, which rushes by a scant few feet behind the house. The lad's body was found two weeks later; his spirit, however, hung around for a very long time. His surviving siblings told me that when they came out of their bedrooms within days of the drowning, they were stunned to see his full-size spirit likeness standing before them in the upstairs hallway. He was engulfed in a brilliant, white light and bore a smile that indicated his utter contentment. In a few moments, the child's shining specter disappeared into thin air.

After my family moved in, strange things began to happen, leading us to believe we were never really alone. One night in the middle 1970s, as I sat on the living room couch after everyone else had retired, I was startled by the sound of loud sobbing. It was like the anguished wailing of an adult female in obvious, terrible distress, and it seemed to be coming from a back bedroom on the second floor. I jumped from the sofa and made the rounds of each bedroom, finding all my family members sound asleep. When I returned to the sofa, the crying resumed and continued for some minutes before finally ceasing. I concluded that the cries were some kind of audio residue from almost twenty years before that had somehow been absorbed by the house via its sheer intensity. Why that ghostly recording was played back for me all those years after is very much part of the unknown.

Years after I had written the initial story, I was interviewing one of Jim and Jane Olsen's grandsons on an entirely different subject. I got around to telling him that his Uncle Vincent's ghost had returned several times, and he wasn't at all surprised. When I described the heart-wrenching crying, he had an immediate, definitive answer. His father had often told the story of how stoic Jane was after her little boy had been swept away by the fierce current. She refused to let anyone at the wake and funeral see her cry, and she never shed a tear in front of her children and their many friends. But late at night, after everyone had long been asleep, her older children would be awakened by their mother's heart-wrenching sobs, coming from what was then the master bedroom upstairs in the rear of the original portion of the house. That part of the mystery was finally solved.

Our daughter Barbie was in high school in the late seventies. Late one night, she came downstairs to use the bathroom. As she approached the living room, she heard the plaintive cries of a small child. She investigated thoroughly and found no source for the sounds. She shrugged her shoulders and returned to bed.

Several years later, when Barbie was attending a local nursing school, the next ghostly chapter unfolded. After the rest of us had gone to bed, Barbie came home late after studying at the library. As she walked into our living room, she looked at a love seat situated inside, and in the dim light, she saw a little boy, sound asleep and appearing very real. Next morning, Barbie came down from her bedroom and asked her mother where Brock was. Brock was the young son of our daughter Diane, and he often spent the night with us. Not seeing him, she was puzzled as to where he might have gone. She wasn't the only one puzzled. My wife, Kaye, told Barbie that Brock had not been here for several days.

Was it Vincent returning for a ghostly visit? That seems like a good guess. His death had been so sudden that his spirit probably had a most difficult time leaving this dimension permanently. The fact that Barbie thought she had seen Brock might have had an even more prophetic meaning. He was himself killed in a horrible car crash in 1988. He was only eight years old.

Shortly afterward, one of our nieces came to visit from South Carolina. Donna had grown up almost across the street from us. At the time, we had a young dog named Chester. He had a unique personality and was a most special pet. Each night around seven o'clock, Chester would walk into the living room and sit on his haunches toward the left side of our large, stone fireplace. As he stared at the wall, he would whine dolefully for a time. Then he would simply get up and move away, acting naturally for the rest of the evening. This scenario played out every evening for the entire time he lived with us.

The night our niece arrived was no exception. As we chatted on the sofa, Chester repeated his nightly ritual. He entered, walked across the room, sat by the fireplace, and whined in a sad and pathetic manner. Our niece looked as though she had seen a ghost. When she regained her composure, she began to tell a story that explained everything.

Donna recounted how, at the age of eight, she heard that her little friend Vincent Olsen drowned while playing on the riverbank. Her parents, wanting her to learn something about mortality, decided to walk her across the street and into the Olsen house for Vincent's wake.

It was at seven o'clock that they walked into the front door, down the entrance hall, and into the living room. A long line of mourners stretched to a little casket situated just to the left of the stone fireplace. It was surrounded with flowers. It was a scene she never forgot. Amazing—but true.

By the way, our daughter Barbie's bedroom was in the rear on the second floor of the original house. She didn't know at the time that it had been the Olsen's master bedroom. More than once, Barbie would come downstairs in the morning with a story that never varied. It always started with a feeling of foreboding when she went to bed. Her room was dark, with the only light filtering in from the hallway through the louvers in her door. She would always see shadows outside the door. Her fear would intensify when footsteps sounded. The doorknob would turn, and she would dive under the covers as the door opened and the footsteps continued around her bed to the other side. They would then stop, and Barbie would actually feel the bed go down as someone or something sat on it. Unable to speak or scream, Barbie would endure the terror as the unwelcome intruder eventually left the bed and walked out of the room.

She says she was never touched by the ghostly guest but was always shaken by the experience, which happened numerous times over the years she lived at home. Barbie's room soon came to be dubbed "the ghost bedroom" because of all the strange happenings there.

Terrible and almost unspeakable tragedy befell our family in late 1988. Our oldest son, Gary, and his wife, Kim, were killed when their car was crushed by an out-of-control tractor-trailer loaded with lumber on a Vermont highway. Their two young children were with us while their parents headed for a weekend vacation on Cape Cod. Meeghan was eight and her brother Chad was eleven.

I was working at a local radio station when Gary and Kim left that day. My wife Kaye recalls that they seemed almost surrealistically radiant as they waved goodbye, heading out for what was to be kind of a second honeymoon. Kaye says the couple had a kind of bright aura around them as they stood in the kitchen doorway. In retrospect, she described them as being "so happy, it was unreal."

Unreal indeed. We learned of their deaths from a kindly policeman who knocked on our door in the early morning hours of the next day. Was that bright aura earlier some kind of forecast of their impending demise? Possibly. In any case, Kaye and I gladly accepted the responsibility of caring for and raising their children after bringing up thirteen of our own.

Remember Brock whom Barbie thought she saw sleeping on the love seat? His death came about just two days after those of Gary and Kim. Those were dark days indeed. Growing up, Brock stayed with us often. He would always watch cartoons on a little pink television set in what I call the River Room at the back of our house. After his death, as I stood next to the TV table and shook my fist at heaven in my terrible grief, the pink television suddenly turned on with no human intervention and began to zip through the channels at maximum volume until it found one running cartoons. The little light on the front flickered on and off like a supernatural Morse code. I knew it was Brock, and I smiled through my tears. The pink TV continued to act strangely for months before finally beginning to settle down.

The following summer, we placed the TV in our camper and headed for our annual vacation along the St. Lawrence River. Brock always loved to camp there with us; this was to be our first time without him, but his pink TV came along. We thought little of it and went to bed early the first night. At three in the morning, we were startled awake when the television turned on by itself at full volume and raced through the channels like it was possessed. We believe it was. We had to finally pull the plug for it to stop. And we had a lot explaining to do to our camping neighbors the next day.

After that, I placed the television set in a box and left it in the garage for several years. Eventually, I brought it to a local repair shop and had the entire tuning mechanism replaced. From that point on, it worked just fine—except for one thing: the little red light on the front still flickers from time to time, as if trying to communicate in that other-worldly code.

Ghosts love to mess with televisions and other kinds of electronic media, and the spirits of our deceased loved ones often insisted on making their presence known in our house through our TV sets. After my mother died in the late 1980s, I brought her old television set home to use as a spare. It came in handy. When our regular console model failed, we set Mom's up on a table in the living room. It was the old-fashioned type that made a loud "clunking" noise when you turned the knob to change the channels. Before long it adopted the bizarre behavior of the little pink one. It had a huge speaker and would turn on suddenly at full volume and begin clunking through the channels. We couldn't lower the volume or shut if off except by pulling the wall plug. We eventually carried it upstairs, where it worked properly until it was later replaced by a modern table model.

We thought we were out of the woods when our console TV came back from the repair shop. Wrong! Chad, Meeghan, Kaye, and I were sitting in the living room watching a special about a haunted hotel in California. In the show, one of the women spotted eyes on a television screen while the set was turned off. It was eerie enough that, when a commercial came on, the four of us began to discuss what we had seen. At the same instant that a telephone rang on the TV commercial, our own phone rang and we just about leaped out of our skins. As soon as Meeghan picked up the receiver, the phone line went completely dead (no pun intended). There wasn't even a dial tone.

As if on a spectral cue, the repaired television console began to rocket through the channels just as all the others had done. It stopped as suddenly as it had started, and at that moment, our phone rang again. No one else dared to touch it, so I picked up the receiver and held it to my ear. Stone dead.

Speaking of eyes on the television screen, here's another true story to mull over in your mind. Do you believe in what has been called "the evil eye"? This one will blow you out of the tub. Kaye and I were just getting into a deep sleep one night in our first-floor bedroom. Kaye was awaked by a nightmare and walked into the bathroom for a cup of cold water. She remained for only a few moments and came out quickly, sheer terror in her eyes. "What's wrong?" I asked. Her timorous answer, "There is a large eye in the bathroom mirror. It is staring at me," was all she could blurt out. She slammed the door and crawled back into bed, shaking like a leaf. Neither of us could get up enough courage to open the bathroom door again until daylight, when all was calm.

Kaye's father, the late Alfred Vaughan, was a wonderful man who could tell the greatest tales about working and hunting in the magnificent Adirondack Mountains.

When he died, I was fortunate enough to be given his old kitchen clock. It was made by the Baird clock company in nearby Plattsburgh, New York, and was purchased by Alfred's father on March 22 of 1892 for the sum of five dollars. I know that to be true because it is penciled inside the case.

As soon as I got the clock home, I worked for several hours attaching it onto the wall of what I call the River Room at the back of the house. I leveled it carefully so the pendulum hung perfectly straight along a line marked on the cardboard instructions inside the case. But try as I might, I couldn't keep it running. Frustrated,

I began to talk to the clock—or more specifically—to Pa, as I called my late father-in law. I said, "Listen, Pa. You wanted me to have your darn clock and I'm happy to have it, but I can't enjoy it if it won't run. If you don't make it work before I leave this room, I'm gonna take it down and ban it to the garage forever." I gave the pendulum a gentle nudge and started to walk away. By the time I had taken three steps, I stopped dead in my tracks. Behind me I could hear "tick-tock, tick-tock," and the clock hasn't stopped running smoothly to this very day.

Soon after the tragic car crashes decimated our close-knit family in 1988, we hired a contractor to do some serious remodeling in the oldest part of our house. He had removed a redundant staircase to enlarge the kitchen and was in the process of tearing out and enlarging another set of stairs rising to the five bedrooms on the second floor. Once the old steps were gone, Gene, our contractor looked up into the dark void where they had been. Needless to say, he was startled by what he saw. His focus settled on the shadowy figure of a man dressed in black, standing on the landing with his hands behind his back as if surveying the alterations. Gene called to Kaye in the kitchen. "Hey, come here. You didn't tell me you had a @%&*@ ghost in your house!"

Gene said he watched the figure for a time, whereupon it simply floated to the right and toward what we refer to as "the ghost bedroom." That night I set up an audio tape recorder in an effort to capture any extraneous sounds from the second floor, but I was disappointed when nothing further happened.

I speculated that the spirit figure seen by Gene that day belonged to a man named Peck who had reportedly constructed the original building more than a century before. I would be remiss if I didn't relay the fact that our friend Gene died of a heart attack not long after the ghostly incident in our house. His son completed the planned remodeling work.

For a time, our grandson Chad moved into "the ghost bedroom" while a new dormer bedroom was being built for him upstairs. After the first night, he got up and asked Kaye why she had been standing outside his room. He said he could hear someone walk up to the door. He could see a shadow through the door's louvers and could hear heavy breathing. The door did not open. Déjà vu. His story was similar to the ones that Barbie had told us years before. It happened several more times, and Chad was none too happy until his new bedroom was completed.

Kaye and I spent considerable time and effort painting and sprucing up the "ghost bedroom" in hopes of appeasing the spirit, but to no avail. Our granddaughter Kelly from the Adirondack village of Saranac Lake moved in while attending a local college. We opted not to give her any preconceived notions about the bedroom before she spent the first night there. In the morning, the first words out of her mouth were, "Papa, what's wrong with that room?" "Why do you ask," I answered with my falsely innocent face. "My television set started acting all weird last night, turning on and off and whipping through the channels. Can you fix it? And my stereo system also developed a mind of its own." I had to break down and tell her about the friendly ghost. From then on, she never gave it another serious thought.

On one occasion, we had overnight guests and decided to let them sleep in our master bedroom downstairs. Kaye and I dragged our pillows and blankets up to a front bedroom on the second floor in the oldest portion of the house. I had barely fallen asleep on my back when I was rudely awakened by the feeling of someone or something on top of me. I instantly knew it was some kind of evil force, crushing the very life out of me. I couldn't breathe nor make a sound. I was paralyzed. Kaye was asleep at my side, and I was certain that she would find me dead in the morning. Somehow, I mustered enough strength to make a slight sound and get Kaye's attention. She got up and turned on the light, and my evil nemesis instantly disappeared. I shook for hours. I felt as though I had been assailed by the devil himself.

Frank and Marge Cluette from a nearby village were among our dearest friends. We were distressed when Frank passed away. His widow asked if I would say a few words at his funeral mass. When I tried to put a tribute on paper the night before, I faced a total roadblock. The man had meant so much to me that I couldn't come up with anything good enough to say. I went to bed with a million thoughts on my mind, but I eventually drifted off into a fitful sleep, while praying for divine inspiration. At about three A.M., I was awakened by the tinkling sound of a music box playing "Waltzing Matilda." Kaye also rubbed the sleep from her eyes, and we could only stare at each other, listening as the entire song played through. The sound was coming from a stuffed kangaroo, perched on the headboard of our bed. The music box inside had not been wound up or heard in many years. I smiled, got up, and finished my little speech for Frank. He loved music and played the accordion. His favorite song? "Waltzing Matilda."

Most of the ghosts in our house seem to be at peace these days, but who knows when they might decide to stop by and say "hello?"

The Ghost of Red D

Raymond "Red" Dashnaw—or "Red D," as he was commonly called—was a beloved man who lived in a little house on Emery Street in the village of Morrisonville, New York. Next door was a long building that had been the home of various businesses since its construction in the early part of the twentieth century. Once a busy local barroom, it was turned into a grocery store and was later an appliance store and a liquor store.

Some time after Red D died, a young couple decided to open a restaurant in the building which Red D used for his grocery store about fifty years before. It was a pizza shop they called "Mister D's." The first time I walked across the street to pick up an order, the woman asked me if I knew anything about ghosts. "Moi?" I answered. "Yeah. A little bit. What's your story?"

She told me that they had come in to work the night before and had turned on the inside lights. Over in the corner, they spotted an old man in a rocking chair, just sitting there and watching them. I asked her to describe him and what she told me fit old Red D. to a "T," wool plaid hunting clothes and all—including the cap on his head!

I assured her that he meant them no harm and probably only

wanted to see what they had done to his old store. As it turned out, I was probably right. They kept track of every time he showed up for as long as they operated the restaurant. He often put their utensils and silverware away—always in places different from where they were usually kept. I urged her to speak right out loud to Red D and thank him for his assistance. She did.

At the end of one particularly hectic day, the female proprietress stepped down into the kitchen area at the back of the restaurant and sighed as she gazed upon piles of dirty dishes and a general mess everywhere from one end to the other. She was exhausted and resented the fact that she would have to stay for several hours to clean it all up. She filled two large garbage bags and walked outside to put them in a dumpster around back.

When she came back inside mere seconds later, the entire place was spic and span. No dirty dishes. No greasy pots and pans. No filthy tablecloths. Every kitchen item was put away (although in a place different from its customary storage cupboard or drawer). Even the stove was immaculate. She looked around, shook her head, untied her dirty apron, turned off the lights, and just as she locked the door, she looked back inside and said, "Thanks, Red D."

The business changed hands several times after that and was turned into a family home in 2004. I think Red D has vacated the premises or else he's content enough with the new occupants to leave them alone.

Pierce's Ghost

What would you do if you were the manager of a convenience store that opened in a converted funeral home and had a ghost follow you into the bathroom? That and a lot more happened in a small community located in the northeast corner of New York State.

I was always fascinated by a large, rambling, two-story red building at the intersection of Route 22B and Mason Street in Morrisonville. Empty and dilapidated when I first moved into the neighborhood, it presented such an aura of mystery to me that I sometimes stopped to look through the windows of the main building and the garages that housed old cars and equipment. They seemed to remain just as they were when the doors were closed and locked many years before.

The fact that the main building had once been a funeral home (with apartments on the second floor) was more than enough reason for the Morrisonville kids to believe that the place must be haunted. And I confess that even I joined the children in the community in thinking that the building looked very spooky, so it was a relief to many of us when the place was sold and work began to turn the main structure into a convenience store. It was good to see the old landmark rehabilitated and opened for business.

But I discovered that the rehabilitation had not banished the ghosts. When I stopped in for my morning paper around Halloween in 1991, Michelle, who managed the store for her brother, the mayor of nearby Plattsburgh, greeted me with her own up-close-and-personal ghost story. It was so interesting that she had no trouble at all capturing my undivided attention.

Michelle reported that nothing out-of-the-ordinary had happened since the store opened a month before, but that day everything changed. Prior to opening the doors that morning, Michelle went into the bathroom at the back of the store. There in the tiny room, she sensed someone was with her, then heard movement that was not her own. Transfixed, she watched in horror as the hot water faucet turned on before her eyes and water began to flow. As she held her breath, rooted to the spot, the handle then moved in the opposite direction and shut off, as if some invisible person had entered, washed his or her hands, then left.

Michelle asked what I thought she should do. She had piqued my interest, so my advice was that she should keep track of any future ghostly activity and report it to me. I tried to assure her that the spirit was no doubt benign and meant her no harm.

Although Michelle continued to be frightened of her unseen guest, she followed my instructions. Each time I dropped by, she added a new chapter to the story, faithfully reporting each strange sound and eerie incident.

Every now and then, grocery items would rise from a shelf and become airborne. Sometimes they would become suspended in the air for a moment or two, then float toward the middle of the aisle and simply drop to the floor. At other times, something would "pop" off the shelf, shoot straight upwards, and fall.

Occasionally, items such as five-pound bags of flour, canned goods, and baby bottles would be propelled through the air with considerable momentum. Once, a bag of flour smashed into a wall with such force that it broke open and spilled across the floor.

The business was later sold to another convenience store chain, but Michelle and the strange happenings remained, and I continued to stop by to hear about them. Items still flew off the shelves, causing concern for patrons and employees, but particularly for Michelle. She was worried that perhaps she was somehow the cause.

Early one morning, according to Michelle, she was doing paperwork in the back office before opening for the day. At about four-thirty A.M., her attention was drawn to a scraping and shuffling sound. It was as if someone was walking along while pushing a chair on the bare, wooden floor. She had thought she was alone; now she wasn't so sure.

Michelle eventually left the store to pursue other endeavors, but I caught up with her a few years later when I started writing this story. She added more details and referred me to other employees who could relate their own experiences. I decided to gather them all together and compare notes.

I first asked a clerk named Melinda if she had seen or heard anything strange. Her words spilled out in a torrent, as if she had been waiting to tell someone for a very long time. Yes, she replied, she often heard strange sounds when no one else was in the store, and there was a light in the rear office that turned itself off when the switch was still in the "on" position. To use her own words: "That light does what it wants to do."

Melinda said she would sometimes stand in the back of the store and watch the front door open as if an invisible customer were coming in. More than once, the glass doors of a beverage cooler would open on their own. She would walk over, shut them, and then return to her station, only to have the doors swing open again. She wanted me to know that when those doors were closed and latched properly (which they were when this happened), they could not open without some kind of intervention.

I spoke to another clerk named Nina. She said there had been so many unexplained experiences in the store that they named their ghost "Fred."

Nina showed me the heavy, wooden door leading into a walk-in cooler toward the rear of the store. It was difficult, she said, for some employees to carry cases of beer and soda into the cooler while trying to hold the big door open.

One evening while restocking the cooler, Nina—her arms full— acted on impulse. Only half-kidding, she said aloud, "Hey, Fred. Hold the door open, will you?" Immediately, an unseen force took the door out of her grasp, opened it, and held it there until she finished setting her load down and walked out of the cooler.

What none of them knew is that, well before all of the events described above, I had done some research on the building. In the early 1980s, I'd interviewed Roy Pierce, a fixture in the community, who was born in 1893 in a house across the street and lived there until he passed away in 1988.

When I asked Roy about the old funeral home building, he smiled and opened a dresser drawer and pulled out some very old photographs. One showed the building in its heyday in the late eighteen hundreds and early part of the nineteenth century. Out front were a horse and wagon, and I could see that a horse collar was hanging on the outside wall. It was a general merchandise store during that time, owned and operated by Roy's father, whose name just happened to be Fred.

You can imagine the surprise inside the convenience store when I told Nina and the other employees I'd gathered together that the ghost they'd dubbed "Fred" was almost certainly that of a man named Fred—Fred Pierce.

But was it? Or could it be the ghost of one of the long-gone deceased people who were embalmed and laid out there during the building's tenure as a funeral home?

As I was interviewing another of the employees, I was interrupted by the wife of the man who bought the building after it had been closed up and all but abandoned for years. Her husband, Herb, had worked there for hundreds of hours after taking possession of the building, cleaning out the old caskets and other funeral home items. His wife told me he would come home night after night and regale her with stories about all of the odd occurrences that happened while he was working there in the abandoned mortuary.

Herb's original intention was to turn the building into apartments, but sadly, his plan never materialized, as he died before the work was completed. It was then that the building was bought by the mayor for his convenience store.

Melinda had other stories to tell. One day, she and Tonya, another employee, were standing behind the counter waiting on customers when something strange happened. Sounds came from the spot where the modern-day cash register was situated, but they sounded for all the world like those that would be produced by an old-fashioned cash register with a handle on the side. They heard the handle being pulled, then the bell rang and the invisible drawer opened.

On another occasion, they both heard the modern cash register being used as though someone was making a transaction—but no one was. Although that never happened again, something else having to do with the cash register did. One morning, the two women arrived for work and discovered that the cash register had been used sometime during the night. A cryptic message had been printed out by the machine onto a length of paper they found in a nearby waste basket. When they contacted the cash register company, they were told that it couldn't have happened. But it did.

Both Melinda and Nina said they sometimes heard voices coming from the upstairs apartments that hadn't been occupied for a very long time. They agreed that it sounded like two people conversing, although they couldn't make out distinct words.

Clerks said the area around the store's counter (in what was formerly the embalming room of the funeral home) had the unmistakable odor of formaldehyde; this, in spite of the fact that the complete cleaning and renovation of the interior had removed all vestiges of the building's former use.

Some employees said they sometimes heard footsteps coming from the second floor; others said they once watched as a coffee maker turned on and off by itself and coffee cups flew off the counter nearby.

After two successive convenience stores occupied the building, it was sold once again. At this writing it is used as rental apartments and the private residence of the present owner. Although he has yet to supply specific details, he has told me several times that he has had unseen visitors.

Perhaps another chapter will be added later to the story of "Pierce's Ghost."

The Ghost of Westland Avenue

In 1998, a gentleman from our little hamlet of Morrisonville phoned my home after learning through the grapevine that I was interested in all things paranormal. My wife, Kaye, took the message and left a note for me to read when I came home from work that night.

Several days passed before I was able to make contact with the man, but it was well worth the wait. He lives in a haunted house. During our telephone conversation, Gary Garrison said he and his family moved to 19 Westland Avenue, on the west corner of the intersection with Route 3, in March of 1998. He recalled having purchased the house from an Air Force family named Hoffman.

Gary told me that there had been water damage in the basement due to flooding, and he had removed all the partitions right to the cement block walls. He put up new studs and drywall, completely refinishing that portion of the Westland Avenue house.

He begged me to come to his home and see if I could help with their ghosts. The entire Garrison family had been terrorized for months. They were on the verge of selling the house and moving out if something couldn't be done either to acknowledge and appease the spirits or send them to a higher plane.

Gary related that in May of 1988, one of his neighbors brought in a giant bulldozer and began to do some excavating and leveling of adjacent property. He had heard that restless spirits often make themselves known when changes are made to a structure or to the surrounding landscape—and both had happened at his house.

The Garrisons had only lived in the house for a month when each family member began to hear ghostly footsteps in the hallway. No one was ever seen making the sounds. The footsteps and other unexplained sounds so distressed the Garrison pet dog that one night at eleven-thirty, he began to bark incessantly. He then peed all over himself and ran into the bathroom, wedging himself behind the toilet. Gary found him there, shuddering all over and unable to get out. The dog had never before acted that way. It growled and bared its teeth at family members as it cowered beneath the toilet tank. It was a while before the animal could be extracted with a lot of tugging and coaxing.

On another occasion, Gary's wife, Erin, told me she was in the basement doing laundry. The dog was with her, hooked on a leash. She listened intently as the front door opened upstairs. Then, there were footsteps again in the hallway. She was certain a family member had come home and climbed the stairs to see who it was. She found no one there. She said she shivered a bit and returned to the task at hand in the basement.

Gary said that within two weeks from that moment, an identical scenario played out yet again. And, once more, no one was found in the haunted hallway.

Gary's cousin Roseanne and her husband Jesse came to visit in July of that year. After the host family had retired for the night, Jesse remained in the living room watching television. At about twelve-thirty A.M., he said he heard someone open the back door in the kitchen and enter the house. He turned to see a dark shadow in the form of a person "floating" toward the sink. As he stared in disbelief, the figure simply disappeared. He said he was frightened out of his wits. He reached over, shut off the TV, and went to bed. He got up before sunrise the next morning and left the house without telling anyone what had happened to him the previous night.

A long time later, he got up the courage to tell the Garrisons about his encounter with the "mystery guest" in their home. And then, it was only because they had brought up the subject of their ghost.

By then, they had named their spirit "George." Many people name their ghosts, and I have had more than one of them tell me that they frequently speak aloud to the spirits in their homes or businesses. I guess it's all part of the comfort factor they've established with their visitors.

On an August night in 1998, the Garrisons were in bed at eleven-thirty when they both heard voices outside their window. They said it sounded like a party was going on. Gary finally jumped up, ready to chastise the partiers. He looked out the window. Nothing. He pulled on his pants, grabbed a flashlight and did a tour of the perimeter outside. Nothing.

Our son Dale happened to be visiting us at the time Gary called and told me about this incident. When I hung up, he was able to add a piece to the Westland Avenue puzzle. Dale told me that his wife's sister Becky lived at 2 Westland Avenue on the other end of the street. He said he believed Becky's family had known the Hoffmans at number nineteen. Mrs. Hoffman babysat for Becky's children at this house on numerous occasions.

I picked up the phone again and dialed Becky's number. No one was home, so I left a message. As soon as they got home that night, they called me back, and all of them started talking excitedly at the same time. I was informed in no uncertain terms that Becky is terrified of ghosts. She assured me that she wouldn't be able to sleep for weeks if I continued "this ghost talk." I suspected that she was curious, though, and stayed on the line, while all of her children chimed in, saying, "Oh, you mean the ghost house? The Hoffman kids always told us that their house was haunted."

Bingo! The house has a history. I told my wife Kaye about the bulldozer work that had been done next door to the Garrison's and she said, "I wonder if someone was buried there?" Others have agreed that it could be part of some ancient cemetery or even an Indian burial ground.

On October 11, 1998, the Garrisons allowed me to visit their haunted home. I drove there armed with a tape recorder and eager ears. I'd asked them to jot down some of their recollections, and we sat down at their kitchen table and talked for hours. As is true in many of the hauntings I have investigated, odors played a big part in this one.

Gary recalled telling his wife that he ran through the house one day trying to find out why there was suddenly a strong and unmistakable odor of garlic. It was pervasive, yet only he could smell it. Another time, Erin said she walked into the master bedroom and sniffed what she described for me as "an old woman's perfume, not at all anything like I would wear."

One time, when the family had to leave for a few days, they invited a male friend to stay there and house-sit for them. His residency lasted only one night. As he tried to fall asleep, there came a loud pounding on the walls that he said shook the entire house. He thought at first that it must be an earthquake, but it persisted. He dressed quickly and ran to his car, never looking back. In the morning, he called the Garrisons and apologized. However, he was adamant about never going back inside that house again.

The Garrisons told me of many instances where apparently minor things happened. By themselves, they wouldn't raise much concern. Taken cumulatively, they spell g-h-o-s-t: like the time when Gary was awaked late at night by the sounds of his kitchen cabinets opening and closing while his family members were all sound asleep, or the scraping sounds they heard from time to time, not unlike a chair being pushed across the floor, or the footsteps in that master bedroom heard by Erin while she worked in the basement.

I left 19 Westland Avenue with plenty of useful information about the happenings there. I rushed home and wrote this story, and when I finished, I called the Garrisons to see if I had made any mistakes.

About a year later, I ran into Mrs. Garrison in a local store. "Remember me?" she asked. "I'm the one in the haunted house on Westland Avenue." "Oh, yeah," I answered. "Can you give me an update?" "Strange that you should mention that," she said. "The moment you walked out our door after hearing our story, the ghostly activity stopped. We have never been bothered once since that day. Thanks you for your help."

My conjecture is that their ghost simply wanted acknowledgment, and after it was given, he or she was able to move on.

End of story.

Ghosts of the Poor House

My friend, Dr. Richard B. Frost, wrote a fine book titled "Plattsburgh, New York: A City's First Century." It covers one hundred years in the history of the city, with many photographs accompanied by educational captions and narrative.

The author sat several times at our dining room table to discuss the making of his book and to select some of my own historic pictures to use in his book. I also assisted in identifying faces and buildings in photographs he had acquired elsewhere.

Dr. Frost speaks of the Clinton County Poor House with its horrible conditions in the 1870s. In an effort to create a special place for the "destitute women and children" living in the poor house at this time, a house was donated and opened on Rugar Street in Plattsburgh. The book lists its mission to "provide separate shelter and care for homeless children who were sharing inadequate quarters with the ill, the elderly and the insane."

He relates that a second house was acquired on Oak Street in Plattsburgh, followed by a move into a larger building on Broad Street. He says that yet another move occurred in 1913. This one took them to the corner of Bailey Avenue and North Catherine Streets. That location is the focus of this story.

At that time, the name of the facility was changed from "The Ladies' Association of the Relief of Destitute Woman and Children" to "The Home for the Friendless of Northern New York." That title still existed when I moved to Plattsburgh in 1961. By that time, the home housed only children.

The stucco-covered complex of buildings at that location is still there, having been purchased by a local developer and rehabilitated into modern apartments. A friend, whom I will identify here as Barbara, moved from the hamlet of Morrisonville into one of those apartments back in 1984. She and her children occupied rooms on the second and third floors.

Barbara's eighteen-year-old daughter awoke one morning in 1985 with an interesting story to tell her mom. At Barbara's urging, her now adult daughter sent me an email from her home in Syracuse. It contains her vivid recollections of what happened to her on that night in the apartment. Following are her exact words: "I remember it being approximately three o'clock in the morning. I happened to wake up for whatever reason. Not because I heard any noises. I had a twin-size platform bed at the time which was pushed up against the wall on my left. At my head and feet was nothing but open space between the bed and the opposite wall. The wall above the head of my bed was where the only window in my bedroom was located."

"Opposite the window, across the room, is where my bedroom door was located. As I opened my eyes, I saw what looked like the ghostly figure of a little boy. I would say he was approximately seven or eight years old. This figure was not solid in appearance; it was more smoke-like. There was no solid mass, but instead it appeared to be almost see-through in some places. It looked like an image that you could place your hand through and never feel anything there—almost like smoke or fog in the image of a person. I was sure that I had seen something, and I was sure it was a little boy. The image seemed to float across the room—not walk. It moved from the direction of my doorway toward the window. Just as it reached the window, it vanished."

"Although I was too scared to fall back to sleep for hours and too scared to get out of bed to wake anyone up, I was not frightened to sleep in my room after that. I think it's because I never felt a feeling of acknowledgement from this presence. It seemed to not be aware of me. My view of this boy was on his right side as he moved and not once did he turn his head to look at me or acknowledge me in any way. If that had been the case, my mother would probably have needed to find another apartment."

"I didn't know the prior history of this building before seeing the image; to me, that rules out the possibility that I imagined what happened because I knew the story about its former use. I also never believed it could have been a dream, since I know I was wide awake for at least two hours after seeing it, afraid to move a muscle."

"One of my grandmothers later told me they were buildings once used to quarantine young children with illnesses that, at that time, could not be cured. And a woman that worked for the apartment manager made a comment to my mother about other people seeing the spirit of a little boy around the apartments."

In the course of my interview with Barbara, as we sat in the Clinton County historian's office, she reluctantly related her own not-so-fond memories of hearing distinct sounds of children playing. She said she would often feel distressed when they "moaned and cried and called for help." It continued, she said, throughout the time she and her children lived there.

Those residual pleas for help are consistent with my own research, which uncovered anecdotal evidence that less-than-savory things had transpired at the "Home."

Barbara told me that she had only a tiny, galley kitchen in her apartment with room for just one person at a time. In four or five instances, she claims to have been startled by the almost overwhelming sense that someone had come up behind her. She could feel someone or something brushing against her back. Each time it happened, she was cooking. When the unseen hand or body touched her from behind, she quickly turned and saw nothing but space.

Was it the little boy from another time looking for his mother? Or was it the mother trying to find her son? We can only speculate.

I went home and eventually wrote the story, then put it aside. Some time later, I was telling ghost stories during a Battle of Plattsburgh commemoration weekend and noticed that a young mother and her eleven- or twelve-year-old son in the front row of the City Hall auditorium seemed to be particularly attentive. As I spoke about the teenaged girl who saw the spirit of a young boy run through her apartment and possibly jump out the window, I couldn't help but notice that the lad at my presentation became more and more agitated. His eyes grew large, and he began to fidget in his seat. He then jumped up and ran from the room.

His mother stayed until the storytelling was over, then approached me as I stepped away from the podium. "We live in that building you just told us about," she said. "We might even live in the apartment you mentioned. My son woke up this morning and found something under his pillow. It was a very old prayer card. He came into the kitchen and showed it to me. We have no explanation at all about how it got there. He begged me to come and listen to your ghost stories today, and when you began speaking about our building, it was more than he could take. I'm sure he's okay. He just needs a little time to think about it."

I took her name and phone number and learned that she worked at the local health department, not more than fifty feet from my office. I urged her to bring the card to work with her the following day. She did, and I visited her at lunch. I held the prayer card in my hands and turned it over. On the reverse was the following: "Saint Marguerite d'Youville 1701–1771. Picture blessed for protection against fire."

The beautiful and serene face on the other side was of the saint, born as Mary Margaret Dufrost de Lajemmerais d'Youville on October 15, 1701, at Varennes, Quebec, Canada. I made a copy of the card for my records and listened as the woman told me about being afraid of fire since childhood, when a blaze destroyed a small store and apartment where she lived on the other end of town.

When she and her son moved into the apartment at Bailey and North Catherine Streets, she made sure the smoke detectors were operational and constantly told her son to be on the alert for fire. They practiced an escape plan in the eventuality of such an emergency in their building. Finding the card gave her the peace of mind she needed. Her son soon recovered from the surprise of hearing the history of their building, and so far as I know, that was the last unexplained event connected with the place.

It appears that our guardian angels are at work day and night.

The Haunted Halls

I've always liked big houses with porches, mostly because I've lived in several of them. There is one such house on the west side of South Catherine Street in Plattsburgh, New York, that has fascinated me for years.

When I was in the radio news business, I walked up onto that porch and rang the doorbell. I was there to interview the man who lived there, who was running for the mayor of Plattsburgh at the time. Telling ghost stories was the farthest thing from my mind. It was also not a priority for Bobby Hall, Sr.; however, ever since I stood in the front hallway, I have felt a certain affinity for that house. I reasoned that it was only because I liked the porch and I liked the Hall family that lived there.

Much later, as I began collecting information on haunted houses in that portion of Northern New York State, rumors persisted about "things" happening in that big house on South Catherine Street. By then, the Hall family had left Plattsburgh and moved south. (They returned some years later.) During that time, Bobby Hall, Jr. remained in town as a city policeman. Another son, Jeff, who was gravely injured in a horrible motor vehicle crash down south, had recently died.

I was reticent about intruding into the family's grief by writing to ask about a ghost story, so I made no effort to contact them. Then, in April of 1997, I left radio and began a career as a Crime Victims Advocate in the Clinton County Department of Probation. One of the first people I met there was Pam Hughes. When she told me that Bobby Hall, Sr., and his wife, Beverly, are her aunt and uncle, I knew instantly that the fates were working on my behalf. She gave me their e-mail address in South Carolina, and the rest, as they say, is history.

Beverly responded with a terrific ghost story. She told me she was glad to reconstruct her indelible memories into a story—and it's a compelling one, to say the least. The Halls moved into the South Catherine Street house on November 3, 1978. Beverly had no trouble recalling the date, as it was her son Jeff's birthday. In spite of the hectic move, they managed to have a small party for their young son. It was also a Thursday night. That meant it was her husband's bowling night. In her words, "A lot was going on."

Beverly said the first five days in their new home seemed fairly uneventful to her, but on that fifth day, she learned that her husband had not found it so. Bob came to Beverly just before bedtime, saying that he had something very important to discuss. He began by giving her "this big speech" about how he didn't believe in ghosts or spirits. He added that he had been shaken to the core by "something very strange." He told his wife that every night he had been awakened by the sensation that someone was shaking him. Each time, he glanced at the bedroom clock and noted that it read four o'clock. He said that if it was indeed a spirit, he didn't care if it stayed, as long as it left him alone.

The next morning, Bob was delighted to tell Beverly that he

had slept like a log—no shaking, no disturbances. The spirit was gone. Beverly, however, related that her night had been exactly opposite. At four o'clock, she was the one awakened by the sensation of being gently shaken.

The shaking episodes were repeated several nights in succession. On one such occasion, Beverly sat up and turned to look at Bob. He had a broad grin on his face. They looked at the clock in unison. It was four o'clock.

Beverly is a strong woman. She was not to be outdone by a ghost, so she decided that she would conduct an investigation. The next morning, she walked next door to a place known locally as "the old Crete house." The Crete brothers were well-known businessmen and philanthropists in days gone by. Beverly spoke at the Crete house with Mrs. Trombley, a cousin and heir to the famous and affluent brothers.

Mrs. Trombley told Bev that the brothers had built the big house for their sister, who later sold it to an older couple named Melbuff. The Melbuffs loved children, but were unable to have any of their own. Almost as an afterthought, she revealed that Mrs. Melbuff had choked to death in the master bedroom at four o'clock one morning.

As was customary in those days, her wake was held in the home, and Mrs. Melbuff was "laid out" in the dining room. She was buried in the cemetery down the street. When Beverly heard this, she had an idea. A day later, she took a fresh bouquet of flowers to the nearby cemetery and soon located Mrs. Melbuff's grave. She gently placed the flowers at the base of the gravestone and spoke directly to the person buried there.

"Mrs. Melbuff, you're welcome to stay with us in our house as long as you like, but you must never bother any of our six children. And you must always let us get our proper sleep at night." She left the cemetery feeling that her message somehow got through.

The Hall family went out to dinner that same afternoon. When they returned to their new home, they discovered that all six of their kitchen chairs had been pulled away from the table.

Strange things happened there almost daily. Bathroom towels would suddenly appear in a heap on the floor. Floral arrangements would be moved mysteriously from one table to another. Small household items would be tipped over or would change places inexplicably. However, Beverly contended that her graveside requests were met, because the family was never again disturbed at night and the Hall children were left alone.

Some time later, out-of-town guests came to visit and slept on the pull-out couch in the family room. In the morning, Beverly asked her friend Debbie how she had slept. The woman answered that she had rested well. "There was one thing, though," she added. "At four o'clock my husband woke up coughing and choking."

Several months later, two other friends came and slept in the same family room. The next morning, the wife, Phyllis, told Beverly that she was startled out of a sound sleep by the sounds of her husband choking and gasping for breath. It was four o'clock.

Beverly said she was certain Mrs. Melbuff loved to see her home full of laughing children. The supernatural episodes seemed to decline as the Hall offspring grew older, but there was another incident that deserves mention. One time when the elder Halls were away, their oldest son, Scott, came to watch the house and care for the family dog. He and his girlfriend, Mary Jo, went to the movies with another couple. When they returned to the house, one of the young men ran in to use the downstairs bathroom. Mary Jo, in need of a bathroom herself, trotted upstairs without turning on a light.

Directly at the top of the stairs, she encountered a woman whom she later learned must have been Mrs. Melbuff. She described the woman as "a small, stocky lady with gray hair. She was wearing a pink, print dress with an apron over it." Mary Joe said that only a small night light was on in the bathroom, but she could easily see that Mrs. Melbuff was floating above the floor. Mary Jo insisted that she had not heard the Hall house ghost stories prior to that night. She ran screaming down the stairs, and it wasn't until much later that she was pleased to have been the only person to actually see the spirit of Mrs. Melbuff.

Beverly told me that Mary Joe's description precisely fit the one given her by Mrs. Trombley years before. She said, "Mrs. Melbuff always wore an apron and loved to bake cookies for all the kids in the neighborhood."

There was a postscript. Beverly and Bobbie's son, Jeff, who died years later from the car crash, had a television set in his apartment. After the funeral, his parents brought the TV into their home, which was then in Florida.

When they plugged it in, it would periodically turn itself on and race through the channels as they watched in wonder. Beverly noticed that among the shows she saw when the channels changed were Yankee ballgames, wrestling, and several others of Jeff's favorite programs.

Beverly ended the e-mail to me by saying "I believe in life after death. How about you, Gordie?"

While gathering information for another ghost story from the

Halls' niece, Kama Stone, I was able to add a fascinating chapter about Mrs. Melbuff. Kama said, "One night, my mother and I were house-sitting for my uncle and aunt and I was awakened by the sound of an organ playing. I wasn't shocked at the time, because my aunt had an organ in the house on South Catherine Street. I then woke my mother up. She was groggy and had no clue what I was talking about. She said it was probably the bar across the street and around the corner. I really wasn't too alarmed until I looked at the clock. It was four o'clock. We learned the next day that the bar had been closed the night before. We asked around and found out that Mrs. Melbuff also had an organ in the house and loved to practice at night.

"Things continued to progress. My uncle's dog had puppies. They all choked to death at four A.M. Some of the family members also suffered injuries in various accidents at the same time.

"Years later, my uncle and aunt moved to another state, and we kind of forgot about their haunted house in Plattsburgh. Then, my eighty-six-year-old great-grandmother became ill, and it was apparent that her time had come to depart this world. I was in Plattsburgh on leave from the military, when it seemed as if 'Mimi' would make a miraculous recovery. We were told that she would be released from the hospital the next day.

"I was alarmed when my mother's phone rang. She seemed to panic at what she was hearing. I asked what was wrong. She said Mimi had taken a turn for the worse. We rushed to the hospital and met my cousin in the elevator. He told us that my great-grandmother had just passed. I got off the elevator and looked at the clock. I wasn't surprised to see that it was four A.M."

Yes, indeed, I do believe in life after death.

Mrs. Pegore's Ghost

Pam Hughes and her daughter Kama rented a tan house on Miller Street in the north end of Plattsburgh in 1989–1990. It was behind what was once a popular country music night spot known as the Rainbow Tavern.

Pam remembers sitting in the dining room adjacent to the little kitchen one night. For some reason, her attention was diverted to the kitchen, where she had a direct line of sight to the sink. She stared with dismay as both hot- and cold-water faucets turned on. Water ran into the sink for a few moments, and then the faucets shut off, apparently of their own volition. She rubbed her eyes, not wanting to believe what they had seen, and being a bit afraid to acknowledge it.

She told no one. But she watched and waited for other signs of ghostly activity in the house. She was not to be disappointed. On another occasion, she saw the bathroom sink faucets go through an identical performance. This time, she was standing in the room when it happened.

Eventually, Pam shared the information with her teenage daughter. They ended up commiserating with one another, because the daughter revealed that she had seen something or someone in the house.

I located Kama in Vermont, and she sent me the following story, which I will quote verbatim: "One evening, my friend and I were getting ready to go out to a teenage club in the area. We were listening to the radio at a reasonable level. When I thought I heard her talking to me, I turned the volume down and said 'What?' She said 'I thought you were calling me.'

"I shrugged it off and had almost forgotten about it until one day when I walked up the stairs, and there in my mother's bedroom was what I could only guess was the ghost of a woman in a green suit. She was shuffling about the room with the aid of a walker. I screamed, 'Oh, my God!' I turned on the light and she was gone. I told my friend and when my mother came home, I told her as well. I also told plenty of others about the experience.

"One day when I was at the home of another high school friend, I repeated the story. Imagine my amazement to learn that she was the great-niece of the lady I saw in our house. My friend told me that the woman was Mrs. Pecore. My friend showed me a picture and I gasped. It really was the woman I had seen that day.

"My mother knew the family that lived in the house before we moved in, and one day she asked Mrs. Pecore's son Bucky about it. He was shocked at the description I had given of her clothing, because it matched exactly the outfit she had on at her funeral."

Kama also mentioned her uncle's house across town as being "famous for odd things happening, particularly at four o'clock in the morning." You've just read those details in the previous story titled "The Haunted Halls."

My conclusion: everything in this world and in all others is somehow connected by an invisible web.

Spirit Piano Teacher and Other Sarah Tales

Almost everyone I talk to has heard a good ghost story from a friend or family member. Some have had personal experiences with the supernatural or spirit world. A few are skeptical and refuse to acknowledge that such things are possible. Whatever category you fall into, I think you'll find this story interesting.

Every now and then I'll find several members of a family who share experiences with me over a long period of time. I write their separate stories and at some point try to tie them all together.

That's what I did in this story. Mind you, I don't demand that you accept all or part of what I say as gospel. I simply relate what was told to me and hope that you read with an open mind, then draw your own conclusions.

On a cool and rainy October day in 2003, I went to the home of friends in Plattsburgh. Sarah Alexander was the eighty-year-old matriarch of the family. Her husband, Eddie Owens Alexander, was to turn ninety on November 1. I'd visited them hundreds of times before and thought I knew everything there was to know about them. I was soon to be proven very wrong.

As we sat around the kitchen table drinking coffee, the subject of ghost stories came up. Sarah began to close her eyes and tell a true story from her childhood, as I sat enraptured. Sarah was born in 1923. When she was seven, for some unknown reason, her father dropped her mother, Sarah, her two sisters, and her three brothers off at the home of Sarah's aunt, Louise Bombardier, on the West Road in Willsboro. They all went into the house except for her father. He simply got back into the car and drove away, and they never saw him again. There was never an explanation.

Sarah's Aunt Louise was known to the family as "Lou-eezy." She was a highly respected pianist throughout her life and had taught piano lessons in her home for many years. Sarah said her whole life seemed to be centered on the beautiful, old piano in the front room.

By the time Sarah and her family arrived, though, Aunt Louise was sick with what proved to be a terminal illness. For about three years, Sarah's mother took care of Louise around the clock. She died when Sarah was ten. Sarah told me that it was sad to lose her beloved aunt and sad for all of them to think that the old piano in the front room would never sound the same again. Or would it?

Sarah's Uncle Mike Bombardier was a railroad laborer. He had to work hard every day to support his extended family. He was so grateful for the relatives having cared for his sick wife that he promised that they would always have a place to live. He was so sad at the loss of Lou-eezy that he kept the old piano locked, vowing it would never be played again.

Somehow, Sarah was drawn to the piano and was determined to get it unlocked. Soon, she discovered that she could unlock it with the key from the top of a can of potted meat. She would sneak in, open the piano and play—first one finger, then melodies, and finally, with both hands, trying to play as she had heard Aunt Lou-eezy do so often. At first, her Uncle Mike was unhappy, but Sarah was the apple of his eye, so he allowed her to continue. He soon was comforted to hear Sarah play, and he finally allowed her to leave the piano unlocked and play it as often as she liked.

One night, as the family was sound asleep in their upstairs bedrooms, they were aroused by the sound of piano music. One by one, they got up, left their rooms, and met in the hallway, almost too afraid to go downstairs to see who had sneaked into the house to play the old piano in the middle of the night.

Led by Uncle Mike, they crept down the stairs and approached the front room. As moonlight sent an eerie glow through the big window, they looked over at the old piano. It was being played all right. They could hear the beautiful music and could see the keys move, but no one was seated on the piano stool. No hands could be seen flying over the keys.

No one said it out loud, but they all knew that Aunt Lou-eezy had come back to serenade them. They returned to bed and the playing stopped. The identical scenario was to be repeated numerous times for several years. Many family members and houseguests heard the midnight music from the old piano in the front room.

The house is still there in Willsboro on the West Road, but it has been modernized, and Sarah says it just doesn't look the same. I wonder if the family living there has a piano. And if they do, I wonder if they have ever heard of the "Moonlight Sonata."

This is—as Paul Harvey would say—the rest of the story.

Sarah continued to play the piano and, at age eighty-six in 2009, still plays for her own enjoyment. Very well, I might add.

But let's go back to her teenage years.

Sarah's Uncle Mike would take her with him to his favorite hangouts and ask the management if she could play a song or two. He liked to show her off. Everyone loved her piano playing and, as she grew older, she would be asked to make return paid engagements. Sarah gladly accepted.

When she was about eighteen, she was playing a gig at a Plattsburgh restaurant called the White Owl. (It's now Mickey's Restaurant on Riley Avenue.) While the local patrons were enjoying her arrangement of Glenn Miller's "In the Mood," three handsome, young men entered the bar and stood by the door listening

One of them gradually moved closer to the piano. When Sarah finished the number, he excused the intrusion and asked her if he could sit on the piano bench with her and play. She agreed, and they performed beautifully together. When she recalled the moment for me over sixty years later, she was still in awe of the man's soft speaking voice and his brilliant piano artistry.

When they finished, he drew a calling card from his pocket and wrote on it his name, his room number, and the telephone number at the Witherall Hotel in Plattsburgh where he and the other two were staying. He explained that he didn't want to be forward, but he admired Sarah's ability and said he would like her to join his trio for a road trip throughout the region.

She smiled and said she would think about it and didn't look at the card until the three men left. The name on the card was "King Cole." She had never heard of him at that time, as he and his famous trio were just getting underway in the recording business.

A few days later, as she was performing at another establishment—this time in nearby Keeseville—the man and his friends came in once again to hear her play. He repeated his offer. She says she was afraid to say yes and declined. As time went on, she began to hear King Cole Trio songs on the radio, and in years following, she heard the velvet voice of Nat King Cole singing great hits such as "Mona Lisa." Sarah came to realize that perhaps she had missed out on a golden opportunity.

I asked if she had saved the calling card and, unfortunately, she did not. Wouldn't they like to see that on "Antiques Roadshow?"

About a year after Sarah told me the story about Aunt Lou-eezy, I sat at her kitchen table in Plattsburgh, enjoying a cup of her delicious coffee. I asked if anything interesting had happened since I saw her last, so she told me a story about her late husband, Eddie Owens Alexander, a powerful personality and country and western music legend in the region. He was known as the Carolina Mountain Boy and performed in clubs, dance halls, on radio and television for more than fifty years.

Toward the end of his life, he didn't recognize many folks, but he always had a big hello for me when I came to visit. Even though he lived a full and productive life, his family found it difficult to let him go when he died in late 2005 at age ninety. Apparently he was somewhat reluctant to leave them as well.

Very late one night, Sarah's adult daughter Angie was resting on the couch in the front room. She was startled by a persistent knocking on their front door. "Bang, bang, bang, bang, bang!" It went on for some time and was accompanied by a loud, male voice pleading, "Sarah, Sarah. Let me in. Sarah, please let me in. For God's sake, Sarah, open the door and let me in."

Instantly, Angie recognized the voice of her father, Eddie Owens Alexander, who had been dead for many months. At first, she was frozen in her place. Finally, she was able to turn her gaze toward the substantial front door. It is one of those heavy, insulated, metal doors with a beautiful cut-glass panel in the top. As she watched, a form began to take shape as if it had come right through the door and stood in the hallway looking at her.

There was Eddie, dressed as he always was in his latter years, in green work pants and a white T-shirt covered with a brown sweater. He was wearing his usual, unlaced work boots. They stared at each other for a fleeting moment. Angie says she noticed the sadness in his face. Then, he faded from view.

She got up slowly and walked throughout the house to see if anyone else was awake. They were all dead to the world, if you know what I mean. Pondering what had just happened, Angie went back to the couch and sat down in confusion. She thinks she might have dozed off. About an hour or two later, she was rudely awaked by a replay of the identical scene—the knocks, Eddie's urgent pleas for Sarah to let him in, and his apparent frustration that the door wasn't opened for him. So, he simply slid right through the door and back into the front hallway again, where Angie got another good look at him before his second vanishing act.

She didn't waken Sarah, but, in the morning, her mother was not surprised to hear Angie's story.

After Eddie died, Sarah was drawn back to the piano. Her children gave her a full-sized keyboard that she kept in her bedroom there on Riverside Avenue. When arthritis began to plague her hands, her friends (me included) and her family urged her to start playing again to limber up her mind and her fingers. She did just that, and it worked. When she played, she felt closer to Eddie. She set up a tape machine and recorded songs over and over again until she was satisfied with the way they sounded.

Sarah plays by ear. When Eddie was still alive and Sarah was stuck for a chord to complete a new song, Eddie would walk over to the piano and, gently taking her hands, he would place them on the proper keys. According to Sarah, he does the same now. If she gets stuck, she simply asks out loud for Eddie's help. A gentle force takes over and places her fingers on the proper notes. She insists that it works every time. I can't argue with that kind of success.

Fast forward about a year to 2005. Sarah called me at home and said she had yet another chapter to the Eddie Alexander story. I hurried over, pen in hand. Sarah had told me many times before that her husband's favorite song was one titled, "The Teacher's Hair Was Red." He played and sang it hundreds of times, both as a performer and around the house.

One day, Sarah started her music session by singing and recording Eddie's favorite song. She followed that with several others. Eventually, she tired and simply shut off the tape recorder. She also turned off the keyboard and walked out of her bedroom into the kitchen to sit to chat with her daughter Angie.

A few minutes later, they both began to hear noises from Sarah's bedroom; it sounded as if someone were fiddling with the tape recorder. They heard it click on and listened as the tape rewound. They sat transfixed as it stopped at the very beginning and began to play "The Teacher's Hair Was Red." When the song finished, the tape stopped and was mysteriously fast-forwarded to the precise spot where Sarah had left off with her earlier recording.

Sarah and Angie went into the bedroom and found everything in its place. They looked at each other and smiled broadly with their special mother/daughter understanding. Eddie must have been happy to hear Sarah do his favorite song and wanted to let them know.

There's more. On another occasion, Sarah, who had long bangs, went into her bedroom to search for something in the top drawer of her dresser. She had the habit of reaching up to push the bangs away from her eyes. As she bent over to look inside the open drawer, the hair fell down, as usual, and she couldn't see. By instinct, she began to raise her right hand to brush the hair to one side. It wasn't necessary—this time. She says she felt a presence behind her. An unseen arm reached around, and an invisible hand gently swept back her bangs and held them there until she found what she was looking for.

Imagination? I think not.

I've known Sarah and her family for decades. I knew Eddie very well, and I know all of the children from their marriage. I also know her children from her previous marriage to the late Napoleon Frank Garrant, known to everyone as "Buddy." I never met Buddy, who died at the young age of thirty-seven in 1955. Shortly after he passed away, his baby daughter Deborah was born. When Sarah brought the baby home, Debbie's six-year-old sister Carol insisted on holding the little one. Sarah was happy to comply. As Carol rocked the baby, she appeared to be talking to someone who wasn't physically present in the room. When the puzzled Sarah asked to whom she was speaking, Carol answered simply, "To Daddy."

Sarah tried to explain that her daddy wasn't around any more, but Carol would hear none of that. "He is, too, Mommy. He right here next to me. Daddy likes the baby. Look, Mommy, he's playing with the baby now." As the new baby made cooing sounds of pure contentment, the incredulous Sarah went over and felt around Carol with her hands to see if she could feel something or someone. She could not. Carol continued the conversation by saying things like, "Isn't she cute, Daddy?"

Sarah was convinced then and she is convinced now. Both her deceased husbands have found a way to cross back over.

In 1970, at age fifteen, Debbie herself was pregnant with her son Jamie. How's this for coincidence? Both Debbie and her mother Sarah were pregnant at the same time! By then Sarah had remarried. His name was Eddie Owens Alexander. Sadly, Sarah lost that baby and was not doing very well in the hospital. Debbie, terribly worried about her mother and terrified to be on the brink of delivering her own child at such a young age, sat in the waiting room. The doctors were inside with Sarah. Debbie was very much alone.

Just as she was close to the end of her psychological rope, she heard a calm, male voice saying, "Don't worry. Mommy's going to be okay." She looked around for the source and could see no one. However, that peaceful, disembodied voice continued to comfort and reassure her, repeating that "Mommy" was going to be fine.

Debbie slumped back in the chair and relaxed. Soon, a nurse came out with a smile and told her that Sarah was out of the woods and would recover nicely. Debbie wasn't able to positively identify the voice she heard in the waiting room that day in 1970. I suggested that perhaps Buddy had become Sarah's guardian angel and had returned one more time to assist Sarah as well as to help relieve Debbie's fears. Even though he died before Debbie was born, both she and her mother now believe it was Buddy.

On Valentine's Day in 2006, I received a call from Sarah. She was so excited she could barely make herself understood. She had walked out onto her back porch and, just as she was about to step down to the patio, she spotted a large heart that had been mysteriously etched into the cement. I didn't have to take her word for it. Her children ran for the digital camera and captured it forever. I couldn't help but wonder which of her husbands was responsible. Perhaps there is a little heavenly rivalry going on. What do you think?

On June 8, 2006, I visited Sarah in her Plattsburgh home. She related yet another story about the spirit of a loved one paying her a visit earlier in the day. As she was sitting in her usual living room chair watching television, Sarah told me that she caught a quick glimpse of some kind of shape out of the corner of her eye. She turned her head to the left and looked at the kitchen table about fifteen feet away. There, crouched down next to a chair, she saw a full image of her late sister, Beatrice "Bea" Garrow Riley. Bea had died on August 12, 2000.

While Sarah stared in disbelief, Bea began to wave one hand with a slight smile on her face. Sarah indicated that she felt like her sister was saying "hello." After a few seconds, the ghostly image of Bea disappeared. In recounting the story for me less than an hour later, Sarah insisted that Bea looked about the same as she did in the last years of her life. She was not at all transparent, but appeared just as if she were truly present in the room.

Bea had spent her last days at the home of her daughter, Rose Wood, and Rose's husband, Dan, on the Eccles Road in Clinton County, New York. Sarah at first speculated that perhaps Bea was somehow calling her "home" to heaven. Sarah was in relative good health for her age and soon accepted the probability that her sister just wanted to offer a greeting. I asked if Sarah had seen Bea any other times since her death. I learned that shortly after the funeral,

Sarah was sitting in the same chair she was sitting in when Bea appeared this morning. As Sarah peered out through the picture window in her living room, she clearly saw Bea sitting in the branches of a large tree in the side yard. The face was distinct, but disappeared in a few seconds.

She asked if I thought she was losing her mind, and I explained my belief that the spirits of our deceased loved ones are always around us. Sometimes the connection is powerful enough to create a visual image, if only briefly.

The concept is almost always comforting.

The Ghosts of Rand Hill

In 2006, I was preparing to record a television documentary during the annual festival commemorating the famous Battle of Plattsburgh, fought on Lake Champlain on September 11, 1814. While on the waterfront, I was introduced to Keith and Carol Lunn, retired schoolteachers in the area.

As is often the case, I mentioned the subject of ghost stories and asked if they had any to share. They did. We sat at a picnic table near the dock and I wrote feverously while Carol spilled the ghostly beans, with Keith confirming every detail.

They built their house at 114 Agnew Road on Rand Hill, only a few miles from my Morrisonville home, and moved in during 1976. The house has two stories, with a master bedroom loft. A custodian at the Chazy Central Rural School had told them that there is a legend about the ghost of an Indian princess who has been seen standing next to a stream running through the old Agnew Homestead property, less than a quarter-mile from the Lunn building site.

Carol said they had only lived in the house for about two months when the strange happenings started. They had two children at the time and both were in their respective beds on the first floor, as Keith and Carol were falling sleep in the loft. Suddenly, they were jarred upright by what they described as a very loud crash. Carol related that it sounded as though someone or something had not only tipped over their heavy dining room table, but had actually lifted it high in the air and thrown it to the floor with a clatter.

They rushed downstairs to check on their sleeping children and to determine the cause of the noise. All was quiet. Nothing was out of place. Their new home had not settled. The walls had not cracked. Needless to say, they were up for the rest of the night.

Carol has an old-fashioned teapot that she leaves on the kitchen stove. They retired for the night on one occasion without having any tea, after making the rounds to be certain all doors were locked and everything inside the house was shut off that should be. Imagine Keith's shock and surprise the next morning when he went downstairs and saw that the teapot was so hot it was glowing. Keith questioned Carol, and she insisted that the stove was off when she retired the night before. Keith checked the stove carefully and found it operating perfectly with no malfunction.

The hot teapot episode has never been repeated. They both agreed that had Keith not found the teapot when he did, damage to the stove and a possible house fire could have ensued. Keith tried desperately in his always-logical mind to find out what had caused the burner to come on during the night. He is still stymied all these years later.

Carol's story continued. As they grew older, the Lunn children were instructed never to climb up into the loft if they needed something during the night, but to simply call for their parents, who would immediately respond. One night, Carol was awakened by the sound of a child's voice saying, "Mommy, Mommy." Keith also stirred at the sound of the young voice. They both got up and went down from the loft to see which child called them. Corey was sound asleep in the middle of his bed, and the baby was sleeping soundly in a crib. They went back to the loft, but the voice persisted: "Mommy, Mommy." Each time they heard it, Keith and Carol rushed down to check on their children, and each time, they were still asleep.

I prompted Carol to try and recall if it sounded like Corey's voice. She had to agree that it did not. It was a young voice, but she wasn't sure whose it was. That scenario was not repeated on any subsequent night.

Just as Keith and Carol thought that the strangeness in their house had subsided, the next shoe was dropped. It was customary for Keith to take off his glasses and set them on the kitchen counter before retiring at night. When he got up in the morning, he would first grab his glasses and then start the coffee.

One morning, he went downstairs, turned on a light, and looked on the counter for his glasses. What he saw was astounding, to say the least, and is one of the strangest tales I have ever recorded. His glasses were on the counter, but they were certainly not all right. The screws had been removed. The temples on both sides had been separated from the eyepieces and were carefully placed in a neat configuration near the glass lenses, which had likewise been removed.

There was no screwdriver or any other tool present—just the parts of Keith's glasses. He called for Carol and confirmed what he already knew. She had not tampered with his glasses, and the children were far too young to have performed this strange act.

Keith had to scrounge around the house to find a screwdriver small enough to delicately reassemble all the parts. He barely got the glasses together in time to head for work, still scratching his head for an explanation. It was not forthcoming.

I asked Carol if these events frightened either her or Keith. She shrugged her shoulders, saying that she never at any time felt threatened by their ghostly intruder.

She added that she felt as though some spirit was merely trying to make them aware of its presence. It worked. She later discovered the spirit was visiting neighbors as well.

One was a neighbor who was a top executive at a local laboratory. He was a no-nonsense kind of guy who scoffed at their stories. As a matter of fact, he laughed loudly at them and said it was all a bunch of baloney. He was soon to change his tune, though. One night, he was rudely awaked from a sound sleep. He was jolted by a strong whack on his derriere with what felt like a two-by-four or a heavy paddle. He accused his wife of hitting him while he slept, and she, of course, had no clue what he was talking about. He walked over to the mirror, dropped his pajama bottoms, and spied a huge, fresh welt on his rear end.

He never laughed at Keith and Carol's strange stories again.

On yet another occasion, Keith's parents came to visit, and the family went to an area restaurant for dinner. When they returned to the house, Keith noticed that one pair of his glasses was missing. A thorough search of the house turned up nothing. They called the restaurant and the glasses had not been turned in. They scoured the car. Again, no glasses. The next day, Keith ordered a new pair and went about his business. Each day for a week, he and Carol looked everywhere for the missing glasses. No luck.

One night, Carol turned to walk into the bedroom on the path she takes every evening on her way to turn down the sheets. There in the middle of the floor were Keith's glasses. They had magically appeared.

After that, there was a lull in the action, so to speak. Carol was feeling a bit less edgy, as nothing out of the ordinary had happened in a while. Then, one of her female friends up the road told her something that once again sent a bit of a chill up her spine. The woman was working in her basement. The metal door leading from the outside was securely locked, when before her very eyes, a complete set of wet footprints suddenly appeared. They came from the entrance all the way across the floor. Impossible? Easy for you to say.

Something else. Corey often told his parents while growing up in their house that he could see what he described as candles floating around in his room. They wrote it off to an over-active imagination. I wonder. Have you ever heard of ghost orbs?

One final story: when they were trying to find a good spot to drill a well on their property, several people did "witching" or "divining" in an effort to find a vein. Joanie Vancour, who had actually taken a course in divining at Goddard College, walked across the floor in the house. She assured the Lunns that there was what she called "a strong force running through the building." They asked if she meant there was a strong water vein under the house, and she replied that it was not water. It was energy.

As suddenly as it had all started back in 1976, everything in the world of the unexplained stopped at the Lunn home. They have been at total peace from the spirit or spirits for some time. But the memory of the things I have mentioned is still as fresh as it was when they happened years ago. Even though I have written more ghost stories from the Beartown and Rand Hill areas of Clinton County, I have not determined what that "strong force" in the Lunn house might have been. Until or unless someone comes forward with more details, we can only speculate.

Read on.

The Spirits of Beartown

The couple that told me the following ghost story has chosen to remain anonymous. They are private people and want to keep it that way. They were kind enough to write about things that happened after they moved into their home in the Beartown/Rand Hill area of Clinton County in 1987.

They purchased their home in 1987. It is a small ranch-style located on a one-acre parcel of land. They learned that the house was built in the early 1970s, and so far as they have been able to determine, no one has died there. As a matter of fact, they bought it from the couple that built it.

For the first several years of their occupancy, they described life in the house as very normal. The strange events began to occur after they had been there for about seven years. It was winter, and New York's North Country was in the midst of a now legendary sub-zero "cold spell." The man of the house was rocked out of a deep slumber by a thunderous bang. It was so loud that he leaped out of bed even before he was wide awake. He stumbled through the house, searching for the source of the noise. He found nothing out of place and no ready explanation. He says he attributed it to the extreme weather conditions, while realizing that it had to have come from inside somewhere.

Later the same year, he was jarred awake by the clanking sound of pots and pans falling in the kitchen. He described his wife as "a master of stacking and balancing dishes in the drainer," and for that reason, concluded that her last effort had somehow "let loose." He wandered into the kitchen for what he believed would be the task of picking up a terrible mess. He was surprised to find the dishes just as she had left them. He searched the house thoroughly and, once again, could find nothing whatever out of place. He went back to bed and decided not to tell a soul about it.

Several times during that same year he was awakened by the sound of the living room television turning on at high volume when no one else was out of bed. He would check the clock, and each time it was exactly midnight. He always turned off the TV and spoke aloud to the ghost, telling it, "It's time to go to bed. Leave the television set off for the rest of the night."

The TV set would seem to be haunted on the days that followed these incidents. While they watched, it would suddenly change channels, then stop on a black-and-white movie. When they switched back to the station they were viewing, the set would simply shut off entirely. Then, each time the TV turned itself on in the night, he found it tuned to another old black-and-white movie.

After the TV mystery stopped, a year passed with nothing untoward. Then one day, the owner was installing a new, hard-wood floor in a basement bedroom. His wife was shopping and the kids were in school. As he measured the next section, he heard distinct footsteps from above. There were accompanying sounds that led him to surmise that his wife had returned early from town. Planning to help her put away the groceries, he walked upstairs. He saw no one and could discover nothing out of place. He descended the stairs again and continued work. Scarcely a half hour later, he heard the front door open and close. This was followed by footsteps around the kitchen. He was certain his wife was now home. The footsteps went from the kitchen down the hall into the bathroom and then into the master bedroom. He finished the piece he was working on and headed upstairs to give her a hand. Once again, he found an empty house.

As he was searching the rooms, his wife's car pulled into the yard. When she came inside, he shared his bizarre story with her. She then disclosed that many similar things had happened to her when she was working in the basement. He pointed out that most of the strange events in that house were what he called "nuisances" or "minor disturbances." However, one of them seemed to be far more aggressive. His wife recalled that one night while he was at work, she suddenly awoke with a strong feeling that someone had grasped her ankles and was attempting to drag her entire body towards the foot of the bed. She let out a scream and the grip was loosened, never to recur.

In the summer of 1997, his brother and sister-in-law arrived to spend a couple days at the house. After the first night, they were all sitting around the breakfast table when his sister-in-law blurted out: "Your house is haunted!" They had slept on a living room hide-a-bed. She awoke during the night to find a "figure" standing in the doorway between the living room and kitchen. She said the house was fairly dark, but there was enough light to see that the figure was wearing some kind of long gown. It seemed to be a female with her hair up on her head. She sat up and said "What do you want?" The figure stood silent for a few seconds and turned to walk down the hall. The houseguest indicated that the intruder was in no way threatening and gave no indication that harm was intended. The female specter never returned.

Thereafter, the house remained rather quiet until early in 2001. The man's job required that he do shift work, so he was away from the house several nights each month.

They adopted a Rottwieler the previous summer, hoping it would become a guard dog for the nights when he could not be at home.

When he was at work, his wife slept on the living room couch with the dog at her side. Late one night, she was awakened by the sound of someone at the front door. She could hear the doorknob being jiggled and turned. After several seconds, it stopped.

The next night, she was jarred awake suddenly by the loud sound of metal falling or crashing. She claimed to have heard the identical sound before, just as her husband had. She was sure it was inside the house but, like him, she was not able to find any cause. As she searched the house with the dog following (some guard dog he turned out to be!), she had the eerie feeling that she was being watched. The sensation was almost overpowering and was certainly most frightening. Somehow, she was able to fall back to sleep, only to be awakened again at four A.M. She said she was surprised to feel that whatever tension there had been was now relaxed and peaceful. She was content.

Their son had a bedroom in the basement and remembered coming upstairs to get ready for school one morning. No lights were on as he entered the kitchen before sunup. He told his parents that he noticed what he described as "a large, dark object" on the floor. It was blocking his way. Thinking it was only their dog, he reached down to move her. There was nothing to touch but thin air.

Almost a year passed without any ghostly activity. The next unexplainable thing happened in November of 2001. The man of the house was downstairs in the basement working on his computer. Again, he heard noises over his head in the kitchen. By then, they had two dogs—the "Rotty" and a Welsh Corgi—and he thought they were playing.

It then dawned on him that the dogs were outside. Once again he climbed the stairs with full knowledge that he would find nothing out of the ordinary. He was right.

Back to work he went, and the house was quiet for the rest of that day. Later that night, his wife and one of their sons went to the stables to ride their horse. He said he was left at home with their youngest son. They retired at nine-thirty P.M. As soon as he had climbed into his own bed, he heard a stereo come on, blasting loudly through the house. He was unhappy, thinking that his son had done it. He got up and headed down to remind the boy that there was school in the morning. By the time he got there, he found his son sitting up in bed saying, "I didn't do it, Dad." The man left and walked into the other son's bedroom. Sure enough, that stereo was on with the volume turned up to the max.

Two days later, his wife was home alone and was doing the family laundry in the basement. As she sorted clothes, she heard what she thought was "a loud rattling noise" upstairs. Fearing someone had come into their house, she rushed upstairs, but found nothing out of place. She returned to her work with no more noises. When the laundry was finished, she went back up to wash dishes in the kitchen. As she proceeded to open one drawer, she was astounded to find that all the utensils inside were scattered every which way, with a large, two-pronged fork lying crossways on top of the silverware tray.

The family's two dogs were kept inside their respective kennels while their owners were out shopping. Two days following the silverware incident, they locked the dogs in and left the house, bound for town. Upon their return, they were greeted at the door by their "Rotty." She was a very excitable dog, but on this occasion, she seemed to be more wound up than usual and very happy to have them home.

As Christmas approached in 2001, the paranormal activities seemed to increase. The older son's stereo continued to flip on at full volume quite regularly. The television was up to its old tricks of turning on and running through the channels several times a day.

My anonymous storyteller says he has pondered their situation and could come up with one incident in the neighborhood that might offer a clue. It has a strange relationship to the family in question. Just prior to the time that they purchased their house, the man's wife and he had looked at an unfinished ranch-type home on an adjacent road. They liked it and told the agent they wanted to make an offer.

Two days later, the agent called them to say he had to give them additional information about the house before they could make a deal. The "additional information" turned out to be rather startling. The couple building the house lived there while it was being finished. One day, the man came home and was said to have found his wife in bed with another man. He stormed out and went to get a gun. By the time he returned, the other man had left. Still in a rage, he shot and killed his wife. He walked into the living room, pulled down a set of drapes, wrapped her body in them, and laid her on the couch. He then got into his car and drove out of the state. He was soon apprehended and was serving a long sentence for his crime. The house was being sold as part of the woman's estate and had been vacant for five years since the murder.

Armed with that story, our couple returned to the house to see if they would feel comfortable inside. Their two sons and a friend came along. As they walked through, thoughts of the murder never left their minds. When they stood beside their car after the tour, their four-year-old son said, "Dad, that house is haunted!" That sealed it. They decided to pass on the deal.

Since that time, they always wondered if there could be some odd relation between the two houses, just a quarter mile apart. I should add here that the original owner of the property where their present house is situated was the father of the murderer. The man who told me the story wonders if the murder victim or some other spirit is seeking solace in that familiar environment. The family members finally agreed that they could co-exist with their "guest" as long as it was no danger to any of them.

Imaginary Friends

When your kids were little, did they ever have imaginary friends? You laughed it off, didn't you? It was just child's play, right? Did you ever stop to think that perhaps those imaginary friends could be the spirits of someone who has passed over? When you read or hear a few of the stories I've collected, perhaps you'll have some second thoughts.

In October of 2002, I was asked to tell some of my ghost stories at Borders Books in the Plattsburgh mall. Since much of my audience consisted of kids in the ten- to fourteen-year-old age bracket, I decided I should talk a bit about life and death before getting into the really heavy stuff about spirits. I asked how many of them believed that something survives after our body dies. A lot of hands shot up.

I told them that many memories are connected with odors. I related that sometimes as I'm driving in my car or sitting quietly in my River Room at home, I smell a White Owl cigar. No one has smoked in our house for many years, but my favorite uncle, Harold Brewer, smoked that brand at his house in Maplewood, New Jersey. When I was invited to spend time there with Aunt Rae and Uncle Harold, I would always see him with a White Owl cigar. He would toss me the paper band from the stogie, and I would wear it on my finger like a ring. He was special to me, and I smile whenever I catch a whiff of that cigar, even though he's been dead for decades. Whether you believe it or not, I like to think it's just his way of saying hello from wherever he is now.

When I finished this story, I looked down at a young lad near me and spotted a tear in his eye. Not wishing to frighten anyone, I stopped the storytelling for a moment and spoke to the boy in private. It seems that as I told the group about my favorite uncle and his cigar, the youngster smelled beer. It made him sad because his favorite uncle had also died, very recently. The man died from the results of alcoholism. His drink of choice? Beer.

Just before my ghost stories to those gathered in the bookstore continued, that same young man asked me to speak with his mother later in the evening. I resolved to do just that. About an hour later, the boy led me to his mother and sister. His mother related a story that caused me to think a lot about imaginary friends.

The family was stationed in England shortly before coming to Plattsburgh. While living in the UK, the boy's favorite playmate from next door died. It was a terrible loss to his family and to her son. Shortly thereafter, the woman told me that she was working in her house and heard what sounded like two children laughing and playing in her son's room behind the closed door. She paid little attention for a while, but finally decided when they were quiet that she would open the door a crack and make sure every-thing was okay.

As she peered in, she spotted her son playing a game. He would catch a ball that came from the other side of the room and quickly throw it back. The ball arched through the air, stopped when it got close to the opposite wall, and returned, as if thrown by an invisible hand. She watched incredulously for a while and finally went in to question her son. His answer was simple. His friend knew he was lonesome and had come back to play. It happened only that once. But it certainly changed that mother's mind about the validity of imaginary friends. And it also acted as great comfort for her little boy.

When our granddaughter Kayla was three or four, I got a call from our daughter, Barbie, on Long Island. Barbie had grown up in our house surrounded by stories of the paranormal, and she was certain I would like to hear what Kayla was doing in her living room that day. Barbie told me that Kayla was sitting on the fireplace hearth, looking up toward the ceiling and conversing with someone who wasn't there, at least in the flesh. She appeared to be answering questions and giving her guest information about her brother and the rest of the family. When the conversation ended, Barbie asked her to relate what had just happened. "I was talking with the man," Kayla said, matter-of-factly. She told Barbie that he was very tall, and he wanted to know if they were all right. He asked about everyday things, almost as though he was talking to Kayla on the telephone. He didn't give his name, but promised he would return.

And he did. Kayla repeated the "fireside chats" with the man for several days. Then, he left, never to return again. A week or so later, Barbie called me in a state of great excitement. She had been doing some housecleaning in her bedroom with Kayla by her side, watching her every move. There was a high dresser in the room; too high for little Kayla to see what was on top. Barbie had all the family photographs lined up along the base of the mirror and proceeded to take them down, one-by-one, to dust them and place them on the bed so she could clean the mirror itself. As she removed one photo and wiped it off, Kayla became ecstatic. "Mommy, Mommy," she shouted. "That's the man!" The picture was of Kayla's other grandfather. He had died of cancer a few years before. He was well over six feet tall.

That should convince you that some imaginary friends are not so imaginary after all. When your children talk to or tell you about another child or adult that you can't see, don't be so quick to dismiss it. Ask questions. Observe. You might be amazed and delighted with the results.

Out of the mouths of babes.

Papa Joe

To say that "Papa" Joe Ribis was one of the most colorful characters I have ever met would be a gross understatement. He was always larger than life. I knew him through his years organizing teamsters in Clinton County. I later chatted with him from the barstool side of local watering holes where he worked behind the beer taps. I patronized his Italian restaurants and discussed our mutual passion for jazz and big band music with him on numerous occasions.

We liked each other and enjoyed many wonderful conversations. Some of the secrets we shared will never be known to others. One thing we never talked about, though, was immortality, and I have no idea about his politics or his religion. Those were forbidden topics between us. But our friendship was special in myriad ways; suffice it to say that we "clicked."

Papa Joe's death created a void in my life that is still present many years hence, and my memories of him have an uncanny way of coming back to my mind. His name pops up in my correspondence with his surviving family members and his many friends.

The phrase "larger than life," so often used to describe him when he was alive, has taken on new meaning since his passing.

Papa Joe has made his spirit presence known several times, in ways that you might find interesting and even amusing.

Patti and Roy Lynch bought his former house at 30 Addoms Street in Plattsburgh. Coincidentally, I've known Patti since she volunteered Saturday evenings as a teenager counting phoned-in votes for the "WIRY Top Ten" music show at the radio station where I worked in the 1960s. Even before she started living in Joe's house, "things" began to happen there.

Before moving their furniture into their new home, she and Roy did a number of walk-throughs. They surveyed every inch of the premises and knew what was where. On one of these occasions, as they moved through the garage to get to their car, she looked down. There on the floor in their path was what she described as a plastic "baby Jesus," where there had been nothing only a few moments before. It was tiny—only about an inch long—and seemed to be wrapped in swaddling clothes. She immediately called the realtor and confirmed that neither she nor anyone viewing the home had owned such an item. She saved it and has kept it in a special place to this day. Is it an icon? That remains to be seen.

The jury is still out as to whether Joe didn't want the Lynches to live there or if he just found it necessary to pull some high jinks on them. In any case, Patti and Roy's three years in the house were interesting, to say the least.

Patti always kept a St. Jude prayer card on her night stand in the Addoms Street house. One day, it was gone. No explanation. It had simply disappeared and no amount of searching turned it up. Some days or weeks later, Patti was putting clean towels away in the linen closet located near the bathroom. Imagine her surprise when she moved a towel that was already on the shelf and discovered her missing prayer card nestled within its folds. Another incident with a prayer card occurred some time later. When Patty's Aunt Midge (her mother's sister) was diagnosed with terminal cancer, another prayer card simultaneously showed up in the same house without explanation.

Eventually, Patti put together a craft room in the basement of the tri-level house. Working alone there one day while waiting for Roy to come home from his job in one of the area prisons, she said she was deep in concentration on her creations. Suddenly, she was startled to feel a gentle hand from behind, touching her right shoulder. Wheeling around in expectation of a "hello" kiss and hug from her husband, she was alarmed to see that no one was there.

Another time, Patti told me that she had purchased a purse, but found it too small to hold everything she tried to put into it. She was in the process of emptying it out prior to returning the purse to the store, when inside one of the pockets of the purse, she discovered what she described as "a whole bunch of gold stuff." Included were many religious medals of St. Anne de Beaupre, whose Canadian shrine is located east of Quebec City. Patti somehow knew that she was supposed to give them to those she thought they could help. She did that and felt as though her mission was accomplished.

On another occasion, a friend had left her camera behind but wanted photos of a retirement party held at the local Knights of Columbus Hall. Patti had taken some photos and later leafed through them to find some from that night for her friend. The pictures were inexplicably gone. In their place were more prayer cards, this time dedicated to St. Michael. Patti had never seen these before and has no idea how they got in her drawer in place of the photographs. The friend who had asked for the pictures suffered from cancer at the time, and Patti had a hunch that she should give her one of the cards. She also gave them to others who were battling cancer. The friends were all most grateful.

In many homes there is a mail or magazine basket on the floor. The Addoms Street home was no exception. Patti was calling herself stupid for having distributed all the prayer cards without saving one, when she looked down at the mail basket. There, on top, was an entire stack of additional cards. She smiled and accepted this as one more "sign."

One day, as Patti was moving from one room to the next, phantom lips blew a strong blast directly into her right ear. She was momentarily stunned. There was no reasonable explanation.

Each time she had one of these profound experiences, she discussed it with her husband Roy, thinking maybe he was behind it. Each time, he denied any involvement. He was as puzzled as she was.

Neither Patti nor Roy can directly attribute all of the strange occurrences in that house to Papa Joe. It's possible that another one of Patti's guardian angels was looking after her. We may never know for sure.

Rose and the Mother of God

Lenore Miller of Rouses Point, New York, was reluctant to tell me the following story because she was afraid of ridicule and because it is so very personal. I convinced her that it is one of the most interesting of all those I have investigated and is far too important not to share.

Lenore was twenty years of age and a young mother in 1977. She lived on what was then known as the Rock Road in Altona. With the advent of Clinton County's enhanced 9-1-1 system, the name was later changed to the Burnell Road. She lived very close to her beloved grandmother, Rose Eurbin, at the time. Rose resided in Mitchell's Mobile Home Park.

Rose, who was in her early eighties, had developed bone cancer, and although she became very ill, she resisted being moved from her home to the hospital. She was a strong, independent woman of unwavering religious faith and deep convictions, and she wanted to remain at home. So, for about a year, Lenore would visit her grandmother often to make sure her wants and needs were fulfilled and that she was comfortable. Her family and friends had been told that Rose was in fact dying, and they attempted to convince her to leave her trailer home for a hospital room. She was adamant, though, insisting that, "I'm just not ready yet."

One day, after she had repeated that phrase to Lenore, Rose relaxed in her bed and fell asleep. Lenore left. Twenty minutes later, Rose opened her eyes and was both pleased and surprised at what she saw. There at the foot of her bed was Jesus—standing, smiling, and without speaking aloud, saying something to the effect of, "It's all right." That was her cue. Earlier, even her parish priest had not been able to persuade her to go to the hospital. Now, Rose told him and the rest of her family that she would allow herself to be moved.

Rose was in and out of a coma after she arrived at the hospital. The doctors said they believed they could prolong her life if someone close to her would make the decision to let them put a pacemaker in place.

Lenore and her mother, Gladys Miller, stood outside the hospital room, discussing the pros and cons of the proposed surgery. Gladys couldn't bring herself to see her mother in such a state and refused to go in, afraid that her mother would die at any moment. Things were apparently dire. She deferred to Lenore about deciding to allow the surgery. Suddenly, Rose came out of her coma for a fleeting moment, sat straight up, and said, "Gladys," loud enough for her daughter and granddaughter to hear. She then slumped back onto her bed.

This was all Lenore needed. She told the doctors to proceed, hoping to keep her grandmother with her for a while longer. The operation was performed, and the physician came out to tell Lenore that her grandmother had survived and the pacemaker was operating as expected. He related something else, however, that she found most disturbing, even as she retold the story to me.

The doctor told her that Rose had been so weak, they determined that she couldn't withstand anesthesia. They made the incision and installed the pacemaker and hoped that she hadn't felt the pain. Lenore was sure that she must have, based on the doctor's description, and she blamed herself for allowing the surgery in the first place. This bothered her for years.

When her grandmother was returned to her hospital room, she came out of her coma, but her mind was locked in the past. She believed she was back in her childhood. Her health failed rapidly. Lenore and her brother, Gary Miller, kept vigil. About a week later, while Lenore was at work and Gary was in the room, Rose left this earth.

Lenore was not at all ready to let her grandmother go. Hoping to contact her spirit, she and her cousin Cathy worked nightly with a Ouija board borrowed from a relative. The relative was afraid of the board and had relegated it to her car trunk before loaning it to the young women. Each time Lenore held the planchette, her grandmother came through. Each time, Lenore would ask Rose if she was upset. Each time, Rose would give the same answer: "No."

Fast forward. Some time later, Lenore awoke in the middle of the night to answer nature's call. The only illumination in the house was a dim night-light on the kitchen stove. She made her way downstairs to her tiny bathroom. Over the commode was a small window. There was no light outside the window and no other light on inside the house.

As she sat, Lenore looked down at the floor. Suddenly, she was aware of a "round beam of red light." It was reflected off the floor and caused her not alarm at first, but wonder. She turned her head and looked for the source of the light. Amazingly, it emanated from an object on the window sill, an object that was most meaningful to Lenore. It was a six-inch-high, cream-colored, plastic statue of the Virgin Mary. It contained a cup in which her grandmother had kept a supply of holy water. She had dipped the fingers of her right hand into the holy water each morning and night, crossing herself in affirmation of her deep Catholic faith.

Lenore took the statue when Rose died and put it on the shelf so she could see it early each morning and late each night before retiring to remind her of her beloved grandmother. The red beam came from the statue, traveled over Lenore's shoulder, and ended by the side of the bathroom sink near the door. As she stared at the light, it began to morph into a life-sized, transparent image of her grandmother. The misty spirit remained there as the incredulous Lenore watched, transfixed.

By then she was so frightened that she got up and ran from the room, not even bothering to pull up her pajama bottoms. She stumbled into her bedroom upstairs and got into bed, her heart beating frantically in her chest. All of the commotion awakened her husband. He asked what was wrong, and she made up a story about having had a nightmare. She knew he wouldn't believe the truth.

Lenore was visibly moved while relating the story to me in 2005. She had not told many people about it over the years, but she was glad, finally, to find someone who understood.

Buried Treasure

Religious medals have been closely related to several of my stories. Since hearing the one I am about to tell, I have carried several such medals in my change pocket every day.

Some unexplained things that happen to people are so personal that they seem reticent about sharing the information for fear of diminishing the profound impact on their lives. Such is the case with this story, told to me by a close friend and colleague in the late 1990s. I assured him that sharing the information might have quite the opposite effect. He ultimately agreed, but chose not to have his name published.

In 1968, a Plattsburgh businessman owned a small liquor store. He ordered a double shipment of liquor and then realized that he didn't have enough money to pay for it. The distributors refused to take it back—and this meant almost certain financial ruin for the store owner. The man was deeply depressed. His religious wife prayed to her husband's dead mother, asking her to somehow intercede for them from beyond the grave.

A short time later, the wife discovered a soiled and tarnished religious medal by the breadbox in their kitchen. Thinking one of the children had dug it up while playing out in the yard, the couple paid little attention to it. A few days later, though, another tarnished medal appeared in the same location, and soon thereafter, the woman noticed a bright, clearly-defined, diamond-shaped light that appeared in the corner of the kitchen ceiling. She checked everywhere and could find no source for the light, not even as a reflection from some other object in the room. At the dinner table that night, she asked her children who had found the old medals. They all shook their heads and denied having any idea where the medals had come from.

The man of the house spent some time polishing both medals. One was of St. Jude and the other was of St. Anne. As he used a cloth on the reverse side of the St. Anne medal, a name began to appear from under the grime. "B-o-u-r-e-y." It was his mother's maiden name. His breath was taken away.

He ran to the phone and called his eldest sister. She informed him that both medals had been buried with their mother who had died when he was just five years old.

She said, "I remember pinning them to Mama's bra when she was in the casket." Soon, the man's financial situation and his depression began to improve dramatically. As if by magic, he suddenly found plenty of money in his accounts to pay every outstanding bill. He gave the St. Jude medal to his daughter. He placed the St. Anne medal containing the inscription of his mother's name on a chain and wore it around his neck until the day he died in 1987.

By then the medal was worn very thin. The name Bourey on the back was just about gone, as was the outline of St. Anne on the front. The family concluded that he should be buried with his mother's medal and one other which he had always worn.

Before he died, he told them that he did not want to be buried with his treasured rosary. He said the rosary had helped him sur-vive combat in World War II. When he found that his illness was terminal, he gave it to his son with the admonition that the boy should use it for prayer. His son told me that he put the rosary away for what he said was "a rainy day."

In September of 1999, the son with the rosary learned that his sister had been diagnosed with stage four lung cancer. She had carried the medal of St. Jude from her dad for a while, but later relegated it to her jewelry box. Her brother told me that this was "the rainy day," and he began to pray earnestly on his father's rosary. A family friend also entered his sister's name into the miraculous medal society and gave the brother a card and medal to pass along to the terminally ill woman. The day he gave those items to her, she decided to take the afternoon off from her job.

As her father had been many years before, she was in deep depression. At home in her bedroom, she began to say the mirac-ulous medal prayer. Finishing the prayer, she felt a need to retrieve the St. Jude medal from her jewelry box. Just as she reached over to grasp the medal, she heard a soft, dull thud, as if something had dropped onto the bed behind her. She turned slowly and smiled broadly when she spotted the worn St. Anne medal that had been buried with her father twelve years before. She said she felt an immediate weight lifted from her shoulders. Her faith was instantly restored. Her soul was at peace; shortly thereafter, the woman succumbed to her terrible illness.

Her brother took the St. Anne medal and placed it in a safe place along with his father's rosary. In late September of 2005, I met with him in my office just before I retired from my career as a Crime Victims Advocate. He sat next to my desk and silently placed a small velvet pouch in front of me. "Open it," he said. I picked it up gently and loosened the cord at the neck of the pouch. Reaching inside, I pulled out an old rosary. When I extracted it from the bag, a tiny metal object fell onto my desk. I knew instantly what it was. I held it between my fingers and looked carefully to find the faint outline of St. Anne. The inscription on the other side had long since worn away. I was moved by the experience. The tiny medal felt warm in my hand. Was it my imagination? I chose to think not. I shook his hand firmly and thanked him for sharing such a deep, personal story with me and thus, with my readers.

Carrie's Flying Files

Carrie Turner was a Probation Officer with the Clinton County Department of Probation on Court Street in Plattsburgh, where I worked for eight years as a Crime Victims Advocate. She told me several stories that left me with my mouth wide open. She has seen and felt ghostly things since early childhood, and it persists to this day.

One of Carrie's stories was of particular interest to me. It is connected with the supposed haunting of a three-story brick building where we worked. It had formerly housed the Clinton County Jail and was later remodeled into the Probation Department.

On Wednesday, October 1, 2003, as she sat at her desk on the third floor, all the files and papers on the shelves next to her came flying off and scattered in every direction. It wasn't as if they just slid off and fell. She says they literally flew through the air and made a terrible mess. At first she thought one of the other workers with an office adjacent to hers had bumped into the wall. She looked around the corner and found that he, Joe Musso, had not moved from his own desk.

Patiently, she bent down and scooped up the papers and files, put them back in order, and placed them carefully back onto the shelves. She then sat down to ponder what had just happened. Suddenly—just as suddenly as the last time—every paper flew into the air and scattered all around her office area once again. I should tell you that those files and papers had been on those same shelves, neatly stacked and unmoving, for more than a year. She picked them all up once again and replaced them. The next morning and every morning thereafter, the papers remained in their proper places. There was no earthquake recorded in the area that week and no "earthly" explanation for the flying files.

It was on that same floor that a jail inmate hanged himself in a cell many years ago; the flying files story may be just one more strange event that was possibly connected with that long-ago death. I interviewed sheriff's deputies who were on the job at the time that the man was brought in after allegedly shooting his wife. He was incarcerated in a cell on the third floor and placed on what was called "a suicide watch." That meant one of the deputies on duty would have to walk from his station around the corner into the row of cells on that side of the building and make sure the inmate hadn't attempted to take his own life.

One night a short time later, as the deputies were deciding whose task it would be to do the cell check, the deed was done. As the designated deputy rounded the corner leading to that cell-block, he heard a rhythmic sound: "Thud, thud, thud, thud." He arrived at the man's cell and found him hanging. His body was swinging back and forth with his dangling feet thudding against the wall.

One of the now retired deputies told me that the sound did not go away for a long time. No matter who made the rounds thereafter, he would hear the unmistakable "thud, thud, thud, thud" just as he turned the corner toward that row of cells. The deputy said that each time he heard the sound it made the hair stand up on the back of his neck. He pointed out that he had goose bumps just relating the details to me decades later.

Besides Carrie's flying files, other interesting things happened on that third floor after the old jail was turned into the Probation Department in 2001. One of the senior probation officers told me of an event that occurred in March of 2002. He went into the bathroom near where the cell in question had once been located. As he looked into the mirror, he could see a male figure standing behind him. This probation officer is a big strong guy. However, he shook as he told me about it. He said that when he saw the figure in the mirror, he was petrified.

Other staff members have related their feeling that something mysterious often affects the electronic equipment on that side of the third floor. Computers, printers, and telephones work erratically or not at all. The stories persisted until I left in 2005.

The original Clinton County Jail that was located on that spot on Court Street was a smaller wooden building in what was then called "the courthouse yard" or "the jailhouse yard," the place where public hangings took place. Research shows that a man named Henry King was hanged there in 1881 for killing a man with an axe. Before that, Joseph Centerville was convicted of murdering his sister-in-law and met his fate on the gallows in 1854.

Even farther back, a man named Francis Alert was supposed to be hanged there in 1816. A large crowd gathered to witness the event. They were cheated out of the public spectacle, though, and began to disburse upon learning that the man had already hanged himself inside the jail. History tells us that the sheriff, not wanting to lose the so-called "hanging fees," ordered the man's body to be carried outside onto the gallows, where it was suspended from the rope in full view.

I would be remiss if I didn't tell you about another interesting story told to me by Carrie Turner. She lives in a fairly modern home in West Chazy, New York. Over a period of time, small items began to come up missing from that home, everyday things like scissors, cards, envelopes, TV remotes, wallets, and the like. Each time something was missing, she and the family would launch an all-out search of the entire place. They looked under tables, in drawers, beneath the couch cushions—everywhere, with no luck at all.

She and her husband began to believe that someone was coming into their house and stealing things when they were gone. That made no sense, though, as most of the missing items had no real monetary value. Finally, in exhaustion and exasperation, Carrie sat in her usual place on the couch and pondered. As she closed her eyes and thought about it, she felt a lump under the cushion on her right side. Reaching down between the cushions, her hand came out with the missing TV remote. She jumped up, whipped all the cushions off the couch, and found every single item for which they had been searching. Mind you, they had looked in that obvious place over and over again with no success.

I had asked Carrie to recount anything interesting that had happened in her house. After she finished, she said, "Does that count?" "Yes, it does," I replied. "Yes, it does."

Set One Up For Larry

Larry Nichols grew up around Morrisonville, New York, and lived with his family on the Flat Rock Road. He was a champion high school wrestler in the late '70s and became a close friend of our son, Gordie, Jr., whom we call "G.R.," through those wrestling years and beyond. Much later, Larry was killed in a tragic deer hunting accident and New York's North Country was shocked.

My friends, Mike and Corrine Giambruno, said they knew Larry well. Mike worked with Larry at the Plattsburgh Lum's Restaurant at one time, and Corrine was manager at the former 8-Post Bar on the main street in Dannemora. She said Larry dropped in about once a week, ordered a can of Natural Ice (the cheapest beer in the place), popped the top, and sat at the bar in front of an electronic game machine called Mega Touch. His favorite game among dozens available was solitaire. When the machine was turned on, it was necessary to push several buttons to bring up solitaire on the screen. He sipped his beer, played the game, usually ordered and drank a second Natural Ice, and left without bothering anyone.

Corrine says the following incident occurred about four days after Larry's untimely death. She was closing the bar for the night and was completing her chores around the place in preparation for leaving. She shut off the electronic machines, scrubbed down the bar, placed the entire row of bar stools upside down on the bar surface, and cleaned up the whole area very carefully, as she always did. She took the money from the cash register and left the bar area to put it into the safe. That having been accomplished, she returned to the bar and immediately felt that something was wrong. Corrine is a very sensitive person and has that wonderful gut feeling about things that enable many people—mostly women—to tell when everything is not quite what it should be. She stood behind the bar and glanced around the room. She could see a blue glow in the front window by the door. It was the reflection of the Mega Touch machine. Not only was it on, but it had been set to the game of solitaire and was operating as if someone were playing. That was enough to cause alarm and surprise. Corrine was very thorough and knew that she had shut it off a few minutes before.

Something else: one of the bar stools had been flipped over, taken off the bar, and placed in the corner in front of the machine. While Corrine was trying to digest that, she looked at the bar. There, directly in front of the machine, was a freshly-popped can of Natural Ice. All she could do was shake her head. She shut off the machine, emptied the can, disposed of it, and put her hands on her hips, contemplating what the meaning of all this might be.

She wasn't quite finished yet, so she went into the back store room to get a couple cases of beer with which to restock the cooler in the bar. When she returned, it was déjà vu. The Mega Touch machine was back on and was being used. Specifically, it had been switched to the game of solitaire, and the game was proceeding as though unseen fingers were pressing the buttons. Oh, one more thing. There on the bar, in front of the machine was—you guessed it—another freshly popped can of cold Natural Ice.

It wasn't hard for Corrine to figure out what was happening. Larry had just come back for a nightcap or two and wanted her to know that he hadn't really left quite yet. She finished cleaning up the area and left for the night with fond memories of that experience and of Larry Nichols. He never returned after that.

Corrine says she always felt strange vibes in the 8-Post Bar. She tells me that for a long time, there was a man's cap in a glass case. She never asked about its history, but she thinks perhaps it belonged to a regular who had died, and someone just kept it there as kind of a memorial to him. I told her that they should have put a can of Natural Ice in the glass case along with the cap.

The 8-Post is long gone, but not the memories of when Larry stopped in for a couple cold cans of Natural Ice and a game or two of solitaire.

Sticky Notes

Dick Coffee was a friend of mine. You might say he was a stickler for details. He was a certified public accountant, used to juggling numbers and remembering important things in his office and at home. He died suddenly, and his passing left a terrible void in my life and those of his family and friends, of which he had many.

I chose that word "stickler" with some forethought. Dick loved sticky notes. He used them as memory aids, and I can't imagine how he survived before they were invented. He had sticky notes everywhere—on the dash of the car, on the coffee pot, on his computer, on his desk—everywhere. It became somewhat of a household and office joke. If you wanted to know where Dick went, just follow the trail of the sticky notes.

About two years after Dick's death, I had occasion to visit his wonderful wife, Shirley, at Edgewater Estates on Route 9 north of Plattsburgh. I was returning some old catalogues and items she had loaned me for a newspaper column I'd penned previously. Having written many heartwarming stories about how loved ones come back every now and then to visit those left behind, I asked Shirley if she had ever sensed Dick's presence there. She smiled. Then, we laughed out loud as we recalled Dick Coffey's sticky note habit. She told me that his office in their home had been cleaned out, and all his sticky notes were relegated to the garbage can.

One day, terribly lonesome for her lifetime partner, she walked out of his office, stood in the kitchen, and asked out loud for Dick to give her some kind of sign that his spirit was with her. Suddenly, she had a powerful urge to return to his upstairs room. As she approached the doorway, she looked down. There on the floor was a large, brand new, unopened package of sticky notes. She smiled broadly as she recounted the experience and said that was all the sign she needed. For weeks thereafter, she would come down for breakfast in the morning and find an occasional blank sticky note in the kitchen.

In 2005, I asked if there were any more sticky notes. "No," Shirley answered, "But when I come down now, I find a few pennies in plain sight. They started to add up, so I got a special dish for them, and each time the coins show up, I put them in the dish. He's still here, Gordie. He's still here with me."

Pennies from heaven.

Spirits in Mooers Forks

The small community of Mooers Forks in the northern tier of New York's Clinton County has also been the scene of ghostly activity. The matriarch of a family living on the Davison Road sat in my office one day and revealed that she had been afraid to go upstairs in her house since her husband's death years ago.

She took a deep breath, and I took notes. She began by telling me she was working alone one day on the first floor when she was surprised by what she described as "a tremendous sound, like someone falling out of bed or something upstairs." I should interject here that there are familiar themes or threads woven through many of the ghost stories I write. This is one of them. Loud sounds from the second floor seem to happen frequently in such hauntings. She insisted that there was no one of this world with her in the house at that time. She reluctantly went up to check and, as happens almost invariably in such cases, there was nothing out of place.

Numerous times she could hear the stairs and second story floors creaking with footsteps, both day and night, and it wasn't just her. During one Thanksgiving dinner, the family and guests were unanimous in hearing distinct footsteps coming slowly down the stairs. The dining room is adjacent to the door leading to the second floor, so there is no doubt that everyone could hear clearly and identify the location of the sounds as they approached the bottom of the stairs. Suddenly, the door was flung open violently, with such force that it crashed against the wall.

One another occasion, as the woman watched the six o'clock television news, the face of a man she didn't recognize suddenly appeared on one of the large speakers next to the TV. The face remained until she fled from the house.

I spoke with her son, who had his own stories to tell. He said he was watching television downstairs one evening when his large, upstairs stereo set came on at maximum volume and blasted sound throughout the house. I assured him that this is also common with hauntings.

Some years ago, I ran a twenty-four-hour radio marathon to raise money for her granddaughter, a teenager named April Lavalley, who needed a lung transplant. Tragically, she died before her new lung could be implanted. I called her our "Little Angel." She was very small for her age, but she had a cherubic beauty that I will never forget. After her death, I helped plant a tree in her memory on her school's lawn. I was also given a copy of her high school yearbook. She was listed as a graduating senior, since the school voted to award this honor posthumously.

It was April's grandmother who told me these ghost stories from the Davison Road, including one about a grinding five-vehicle crash near North Hudson, New York, in 1999. The airbags deployed, and those in the car with her were gasping for breath, frightened that they would all die. They mistook the powder from the airbags for smoke in the car and imagined a fire. A moment later, the grandmother glanced to her right. There on the back seat with her was none other than April in her spirit form. April's face was calm and her voice was clear and soothing as she said "You're all right, Meme. You're gonna be all right." And they were. The vehicle was mangled, but no one sustained a scratch.

The Ghost of North Catherine Street

Al and his wife, Amelia "Smokey" Hassler, told me that, in 1969, they had purchased an old house at 26 North Catherine Street in Plattsburgh, across from what was then known as Mount Assumption Institute (or MAI), a Catholic parochial high school. The school was expanded and eventually became Seton Catholic Central School. Seton eventually moved to the former Plattsburgh Air Force Base property.

The original school was built on a sand ridge of land that had much earlier gained the nickname "Hanging Hill." Six months prior to the famous naval "Battle of Plattsburgh" on Lake Champlain in 1814, a British spy named William Baker was executed there by way of a public hanging. It was not at all uncommon for people to come from far and wide to gawk at the tall, wooden gallows as a convicted person dangled from the end of a rope until dead. It was thought that making such executions into public spectacles would act as a deterrent to crime.

Apparently Baker's ghost lingered in the area for many years. There was a legend created by boys who would frequent the hill after the hanging. They would approach the spot where the gallows had stood and would call out something like, "Baker, for what was you hung?" They soon learned that if they repeated that question three times and stopped to listen intently, they could hear a slow but clear and eerie response: "Nothing."

Passing the legend of Baker's ghost down from generation to generation, boarding students at MAI often told their school administrators that they saw or heard things in their building or on the school grounds that indicated to them that William Baker had not totally "passed over."

The Hassler's house, which they purchased from Dr. Carl Englehart in June of 1969, was the site of some rather frightening happenings during their occupancy. There were two apartments in the house. One of them was upstairs where the Hassler family lived with their daughters, Kim and Allison, and son, Albert. Another family lived in the first floor apartment.

Allison slept in a small bedroom near the top of the stairs in that North Catherine Street house. She says one incident particularly stuck in her mind. One night she awoke and got up to find something to drink. She left her bedroom without turning on any lights and felt her way down the stairs and through the living room, which led to the dining room. Beyond that was the kitchen. She said she noticed what she described as "a kind of white film across the doorway between the living and dining rooms." Dismissing it as some kind of weird anomaly, she passed through it and immediately felt very cold air in that spot. She remembers seeing nothing else out of the ordinary that night. However, she claims to have seen the ghost of a "scary man" in that apartment on several occasions thereafter.

About a year later, when Allison was a young adult, her friend Ruth "Ruthie" Loughan came over to spend the night. Ruthie got up from a trundle bed in the middle of the night to use the bathroom. She swears she saw "the gruesome face of a man" in the ceiling over the bed as she looked up. Petrified, she ran into the bathroom and shut the door. When Allison noticed that her friend had not returned right away, she got up herself and knocked on the bathroom door. She asked Ruthie if everything was okay. Through the door, Ruthie related what she had just seen.

Allison, hoping to reassure Ruthie, said she had seen the face many times, and he really wasn't as unfriendly as he appeared. She told her friend that there was nothing to worry about. It was too late. Ruthie could not be comforted for a very long time. Eventually, she ventured out of the bathroom and went back to bed without further incident.

The late Smokey Hassler said that when her family moved into the building, they discovered funeral supplies in the basement. There were embalming fluids and other items, and there was also a crib-like device used to hold the remains of babies that had died. There was a funeral home nearby, on the corner of Brinkerhoff and North Catherine Streets, that later became a bed and breakfast. The funeral home was operated by John O'Neil, who at one time was said to have lived with his family in the 26 North Catherine Street residence. Mrs. Hassler also told me that a local funeral home stored caskets in the barn out back of the North Catherine Street house while they were living there.

Smokey's husband, Al, a retired teacher from Plattsburgh State University, chimed in, saying that he had also seen a ghost in the house. He said that he came home late one night from playing hockey in a men's league. He was about to mount the stairs to their apartment when he looked up and saw the full figure of a man dressed in dark clothing at the head of the stairs. Al said he was rather nonchalant at the time, explaining to me later that his family had become "rather used to the ghost." It didn't really threaten anyone. So, he shrugged his shoulders and started up the stairs. By the time he reached the top, the ghostly figure had vanished, but he reported feeling "icy cold" when he passed through the spot where the spirit had stood only moments before.

I learned much later that several additional occupants of that house on North Catherine Street before and after the Hasslers had similar encounters with "the man."

I was told that one family went so far as to engage the services of a local priest to come in and try to exorcise the place. It must have worked, because I have not heard of any more sightings for several years.

Could the Hasslers and others have been introduced to the spirit of hanged spy William Baker, who met his demise on "Hanging Hill," or was their ghost a remnant of some long-ago funeral next door? Ah, that is the question.

Bill Hogan's Ghost

For years, I've heard stories about the ghost of an old farmer who lived not a half mile from my Morrisonville home. He is said to have haunted at least one family whose house was built on the exact spot where he died many years before. A lifelong friend who also lives in our community gave me scant details, but my appetite for such delicious tidbits was whetted and the search was on.

The woman chose not to be publicly identified, but I know her to be trustworthy and honest. Her son and daughter-in-law lived in the house in question and were bothered often by the old farmer's ghost. I started digging and learned that a local fireman named Herb Farrell, Jr., might be able to give me some background. I hit the jackpot. I called Herb and asked if he could recall the farmer's name. "Recall?" he exclaimed. "That was one of the scariest things that ever happened to me!"

I was off and running, my sharpened pencil copying down everything Herb said. Here's how it went: "I believe it was 1969. I was a brand new recruit in the Morrisonville Volunteer Fire Department. The fire siren rang and I heard there was a grass fire on Beckwith Street, up on the hill just off Route 22B, not far from where I lived. When I got up there, Bud Rock was already on the scene and hollered for me to 'Get that booster reel up here right now!' I struggled up the steep grade and was astonished to see a man lying on his back. His bib overalls had already started to burn through and his big, blue eyes were staring up at me. Bud kept saying 'Hose him down. Hose him down.' But it was too late, the poor man was already dead. He was in his mid-seventies, as I remember, and burned his fields like that every year. This time, though, he apparently had a heart attack or something and fell down, right into the fire."

Herb went on to say that the farmer, Bill Hogan, was found on a flat area at the top point of the hill. It was such a frightening experience for the new fireman that he dropped his hose and began to run toward the village. He didn't stop until he arrived at the fire station, almost a half mile away. Herb said he couldn't eat or sleep for three days. The image of poor Bill Hogan filled his mind 24/7. "Even now," Herb added, "over thirty years later, I can still see those blue eyes staring up at me as if it were yesterday." He laughed, though, when recalling that the older fireman had been merciless in their teasing of the new recruit for months after the event.

Everybody knew kindly Bill Hogan, according to Herb. Bill lived in the big, red brick house that still stands on the property, which has now been turned into a housing development. He had a beautiful team of horses and never owned a tractor. He brought his loose hay in from his fields with the team and used an old, junked car to pull the hay into his barn. Bill's wife, who was a local schoolteacher, later sold the property to the developer.

Ironically, the son of the woman who told me the initial story built his new home over the precise spot where the farmer's body was found. His brother's family also moved into the development, and all of them began to notice strange happenings inside and outside that house. Bill Hogan's ghost was often seen, standing or walking around aimlessly. He appeared to be confused and would stop, put his hands in the pockets of his overalls, and look around, as if perplexed at what he saw. The old farmer never bothered anybody in life and certainly didn't threaten anyone after his death. As soon as the new residents of the development heard of Bill's untimely demise, they were most tolerant of his perpetual wanderings.

May his soul someday rest in peace.

The Ghost of the Gale

As I shared a meal with a friend and his wife in 1997, he suggested that I write a story about the ghost of Uncle Pete. I asked if he was referring to the late Pete Trudo from Jericho in the Clinton County town of Altona. When he answered in the affirmative, I wondered how in the world he would know anything of Pete Trudo, much less know tales about his ghost that even I didn't know.

Pete Trudo was my wife Kaye's uncle. The house being discussed at the dinner table was the scene of Kaye's birth. As a matter of fact, her mother, the late Leona Trudo Vaughan, was born there in the year 1900. My friend's connection was with a YMCA day camp that was later built on the property; he said the ghost of Uncle Pete had become a legend among the campers and counselors there. It was difficult to pin down anything specific that had happened at the camp, but the stories that were perpetuated around their nightly campfires became embellished almost beyond belief.

The old, two-story, wood frame house where my wife and her mother were born has long since been torn down and taken away, but while it was there, it was the stuff great stories are made of.

In the late nineteenth and early twentieth centuries, the farm was known as "Gale Meadows." I have a post card advertising it as "a fine dairy farm producing the sweetest butter along with maple syrup in season." In later years, the name was shortened simply to "The Gale." I am told that the Gale family owned the property before young Bill Trudo and his wife, the former Lizzie Gardner, bought it sometime in the last decade of the 1800s.

I was amused to learn, while researching the ghost stories and the family tree, that Bill Trudo was considered a psychic in his day. More than once, he somehow knew when people in his area had died. Somehow, the information got into his head without the benefit of a telephone, radio, television, computer, or even electricity. They didn't get a newspaper regularly, nor did they have anything but sporadic mail delivery. Their only contact outside their immediate family and close neighbors was at church on Sunday and their infrequent visits to the stores in Plattsburgh.

There is a story about old Bill Trudo that bears repeating. It has to do with one of his friends who died. Bill didn't bother going to the man's funeral and was chided by another friend a few days later. The friend asked Bill why he had failed to take the time to pay his respects. Bill replied matter-of-factly that he was too busy working with his team in the fields and couldn't get away for the wake or funeral. The man was not at all happy with what he considered a lame excuse and told Bill that when it was his time to leave the earth, he would guarantee that Bill wouldn't be working in the fields.

It later came about exactly that way. Bill was in the fields doing work one day. His team reared up and refused to do another lick of work. Frustrated and angry, Bill returned to the house, put the horses away, and told Lizzie that there was no use trying to get anything more done. He knew that somebody had died.

A few hours later, a neighbor arrived at Bill's house to tell him that the friend who had made the earlier prediction had indeed passed away, at precisely the time Bill had been out in the fields working and his horses rebelled. Thereafter, Bill Trudo never again missed the wake and funeral of a friend. Family members related to me that each time there was a death, old Bill would come in from the fields, put the team away, and tell Lizzie that it was no use trying to work any more. He could even tell her who had died. Sooner or later, he would get the official word on the passing and would make his appearance on behalf of the survivors.

Bill Trudo died of throat cancer in that house in about 1917. His son, Pete, took over the farm and operated it until his death in 1945 at Champlain Valley Hospital in Plattsburgh. The old house stood vacant until the land was purchased by the local YMCA for their day camp. It was bought from a relative named Roy Lagoy in 1965 and soon became known as "Camp Jericho."

Soon after, Gary Walker moved into the house to help with remodeling work. He said he tore out the ancient wiring upstairs and installed an indoor bathroom, the first ever indoor plumbing in the house. It was during that time period that the ghost really began to make itself known. They would hear strange sounds at night along with footsteps in the house when no one else was around. After he installed electricity in a few rooms, he said lights would turn on and off by themselves. They were never really afraid of the ghost—just fascinated by the otherworldly events.

There were published newspaper articles that added some

credence to the ghost stories. In one of them, the wife of the man who asked me to write about the ghost of Uncle Pete told the Press about a number of incidents. One night, she had a girlfriend staying overnight with her in the house. They arrived there at about one in the morning, and as they drove down the long dirt driveway, they remarked that all the lights were on inside the house. No lights had been on when they left the house several hours before.

Another time, the horn on the YMCA bus began to mysteriously blow at five o'clock one morning. No one else was around. The woman further said that she felt a presence in the house with her on many occasions, and she often felt a rush of cold air at the same time.

She had television problems, too. Her set would sometimes turn itself on. Her dog often chased something throughout the house that no one else could see. Each time the dog and the invisible guest would pass in front of the TV, the signal "would go haywire."

She and her husband both told me that while they lived in the old house, their dog went missing. They searched the entire farm property unsuccessfully, and could find no sign of their pet. Three months later, shortly after they finished their work in the house and moved out, the dog was located far away and returned to them under circumstances that they both described as nothing less than miraculous.

On one occasion, the woman said her husband was shooting arrows at a barn on the property. Later that night, all sorts of strange things happened to them inside the house. She always blamed it on Uncle Pete. She reasoned that he just wanted to make sure nobody damaged anything on the property.

A former YMCA director indicated to me that the odd events didn't seem to start until the "Y" took ownership of the property. That confirms what I was able to learn from my friends who lived in and worked on the old house at that time.

There was another story about three Air Force servicemen who drove to the house for an overnight stay. They never made it through the night. Before morning, they were so spooked by the ghost that they showed up at the "Y" director's house in the middle of the night. Two of the men were electricians and the third was an electronics technician. They insisted that a light suddenly turned on in one of the rooms that had no electricity at the time. When that happened, they gathered their things and left.

The director said that was about the time people starting calling the ghost Uncle Pete. They had no idea there had ever been a man named Pete Trudo. Pete was just a name that popped into someone's head and it stuck. They told all the youngsters who attended the day camp that Uncle Pete was a friendly ghost who was just watching over the place, kind of like a caretaker. He convinced them that Uncle Pete wouldn't hurt a fly. If indeed the ghost there is of Uncle Pete, the director was certainly right about one thing. Everyone I spoke with who knew him in life described Pete Trudo as a kind and wonderful person.

Two reporters from the Plattsburgh Press-Republican newspaper agreed to take a dog along and spend the night in the old house at Camp Jericho around Halloween one year. Although the women didn't encounter any ghosts, one of the reporters told me she had the best sleep in years that night. Meanwhile, the other woman claimed to have felt something gently tugging on her bed during the night. Neither could agree on whether it was the ghost of Uncle Pete or their very real dog, Buddy. The next morning, while driving back to Plattsburgh, they listened to me broadcasting on the local radio station. They joked that Pete didn't show up while they were there because he was old fashioned and "didn't believe in getting intimate on the first date."

Since first writing this story, I have been able to add stories from folks who later offered their recollections. Hunters walking through the area claim to have seen lights on in the house long after the electricity had once again been cut off. One man told me he saw a single light on and walked up to the house to investigate, only to find no one there.

The present YMCA director has also told me of hearing strange sounds in and around the day camp building. He is not the least bit superstitious, but he says, "One has to wonder." Indeed. Could the ghost be that of old Bill Trudo rather than his son Pete? Or were they right when they put a name to the spirit many decades ago?

I am told that there was another house on the Gale Meadows farm in the early days, where Bill's oldest son, Charlie, lived at one time. A Trudo relative told me a story that should be added here. Sometimes in the basement of Charlie's house, they could hear what sounded for all the world like a baby's plaintive cries. Each time the crying started, they would go down cellar and look around. Each time, they came back with no explanation for the sounds.

Years later, when foundation work was being undertaken to make alterations in the cellar, workman came across a tiny skeleton. Authorities were notified and confirmed that the baby had died a long time before it was discovered. They explained that it was not uncommon to bury stillborn babies in the dirt basements of area homes. A pink bow and a tiny silver ring were found between the foundation stones. That, also, was said to have been a fairly common practice many years ago. The family reportedly had the baby's bones blessed and buried in the nearby Altona Cemetery. The crying ceased with the baby finally at rest.

Mrs. Kilfoyle, Where Are You?

I learned early on in my quest for ghost stories that a haunted house doesn't always look haunted from the outside. It's generally what is happening inside that counts. That fact was brought home to me when a young man sat in my office back in September of 2001 and told me a story that caught my attention from beginning to end.

Nineteen-year-old Travis Sears had never thought much about ghosts until 1998, when he moved with his dad into a house at 2534 Route 3 in Cadyville, New York, that was formerly owned by a family named Kilfoyle. From the outside, the place looks like a fairly average, white, two-story, wood-frame structure. Travis liked his new home, and his dad was especially attracted to it. He said the house was built exactly like his own parents' home. He made an immediate connection: the house "felt good" to him.

For nine months or so, everything seemed just fine. Then it started. One night, Travis was sitting alone in the living room watching television. Suddenly, above the sound of the TV, he heard what he described as fast-paced running upstairs, like two children chasing each other from room to room. The footsteps would stop momentarily, and he could hear what sounded like children laughing and giggling, as if they were playing hide and seek. Running. Giggling. The scenario was played out twice that night. Travis said that, each time, he would instantly punch the "mute" button on his television remote, thinking that he had inadvertently left an upstairs radio playing. He hadn't; when he heard the running and giggling a second time, he realized that he was not alone in the house.

Three weeks later, it happened again. This time, Travis was sitting in the dining room looking through the archway at the same television in the adjacent living room. He didn't hear running, but he could easily pick up on the sound of children's laughter and excited conversation, although he wasn't able to hear distinct words. Shortly thereafter, Travis's dad removed the door at the foot of the stairs to aid in heat circulation in the house. From that moment, the running and giggling upstairs ceased.

The next unexplained incident happened in the fall of 1999. Travis and two of his friends were returning to the Cadyville house at around ten P.M. As they drove down the hill and around the corner, they had a full view of the building. Travis said neither he nor his father ever pulled the dining room curtains open. They were always left closed. His dad wasn't home that night, but all three teens in the car could see that someone appeared to be holding the curtain completely back on one side. Further, the boys could see a light on in the dining room behind the curtain. Travis remembers saying to his friends, "Hey, somebody's home."

As they drove closer, the light in the dining room seemed to fade and the room grew dark. They parked the car and Travis went inside. He flipped on the dining room light and glanced toward the curtain. It was tightly closed.

The boys were planning a camping trip, and Travis was stopping by to grab some blankets. Just as he grabbed the covers, he heard the car horn sounding outside. Trotting out to see what was up, his friends told him about a weird experience that happened moments before. They had been sitting in the car with the door open. All of them could hear what sounded like children running through the back corner of the yard, laughing as they went. They said they were spooked and shut the car door, starting the engine and blasting the horn for Travis. Travis said that after that, his buddies were not at all anxious to return to the house on Route 3 in Cadyville.

Things were fairly uneventful for about six months. Then, one evening, Travis was headed home from work at a local grocery store, when he drove around the corner and glanced at the house. Déjà vu! The dining room light was on and the curtain was being held all the way back on one side by some unseen force. With no small amount of trepidation, he entered the dining room. The light was off and the curtain had returned to normal.

About a month later, Travis heard something that seemed to explain what he'd seen. His dad was told by a neighbor that the dining room window was the late Mrs. Kilfoyle's favorite place to sit. She spent most of her time there, holding the curtain back and watching the people next door as they worked outside. As a matter of fact, Mrs. Kilfoyle was sitting by that window when she died.

When Travis heard the story of Mrs. Kilfoyle, his fear was gone. Never thereafter did either he or his dad feel threatened by the spirit or spirits in their house. They said they just acknowledged that they were not alone and went about their daily lives.

Mrs. Kilfoyle—if indeed the spirit was that of Mrs. Kilfoyle—

seemed to be a woman who had to have everything in its proper place, especially in the refrigerator. Three or four times after moving into the Cadyville house, both Travis and his dad had been conscious of a light in the corner of their eyes while they watched television in the living room at night. They were aware that it was the tiny bulb inside their kitchen refrigerator. As they craned their necks and looked over into the kitchen, they were astounded to see the refrigerator door swing open, then close slowly—but not completely. The first few times it happened, they both got up and went into the kitchen to investigate further. They were surprised to find that objects inside their fridge had been rearranged. For example, the catsup bottle, which they had always kept on the door, was moved to the far rear of a bottom shelf.

Travis told me that he and his dad always entered their home through the kitchen door, which had a screen door that made a distinctive sound. Often, when they were sitting in the living room, they heard the screen door in the kitchen as it opened and closed, and when it swung all the way open, they heard the "slap" as it struck the slanted wooden brace holding up the back porch. They would turn and wait to see who was coming to visit, but no one could ever be seen.

Travis's father related as many stories about the house as his son did. He claimed that, when he was "alone" in the house, he often heard sounds like someone was home besides him. More than once he called out, thinking Travis had returned from work in the early morning. There was never an answer. They both wondered if Mrs. Kilfoyle was looking after the happy spirit children or if she just wanted to make sure her house was being well taken care of.

The Ghost of Farmer John

In 2000, I was told about Ernie Dubrey and his haunted farmhouse on the Chazy Lake Road in the Town of Saranac. It took me a while, but I finally located Ernie. He told me that his wife of many years died in 1986, and he had turned the farm over to his son Douglas, who continued to live in the house.

Ernie was seventy-four when we first spoke by phone, but we felt as though we had been friends forever. He's that kind of guy. He learned the value of a buck early in life, scrounging for everything he ever had. You learn to scrounge, Ernie said, when you're one of eleven children. He began making money as a barber at the tender age of thirteen. He left for a stint in the United State Navy, then came back home to cut hair in his hometown for two more decades.

As if that weren't enough, Ernie also worked a while for the United Parcel Service, operated a cleaning business, tried his hand at farming, and was in charge of the Saranac Recreation Park for eighteen years. He told me that he bought the farm at 262 Chazy Lake Road in 1961 for $6,000. For Ernie, it was a dream come true. Ten years earlier, as he and his wife drove past the place, he informed his spouse emphatically that they would live there someday. He later said that he couldn't put his finger on it at the time, but he "just knew" that owning the home and property was somehow inevitable.

There was a catch. When he inquired about it, he learned that the owner, John Bruce, wasn't ready to sell. But Ernie was his barber, so every time Bruce came in for a haircut, Ernie tried to make a deal. For a long time, it just wasn't happening. Finally, out of the blue, Bruce came in one day and said, "Ernie, if you're still interested, you can have the farm." Those words were music to Ernie's ears. A deal was struck in February of 1961. Ernie wanted to move in right away, but that was impossible. The interior of the house was in rough shape. There was much to be done by way of painting, papering, and repairing. Ernie wanted it to be just right for his family.

Ernie searched the deed back to 1841 and learned that their home began as a one-story farmhouse. Some years after it was built, a half story was added; in 1921, an old granary was moved from elsewhere on the property and attached to the house. The farm itself was also pieced together like a patchwork quilt over the years, eventually totaling 167 acres.

Ernie and his wife were so happy when they were finally able to move in. It wasn't long, though, before strange and unexplainable things began to happen there. Their youngest son even tried to run away from home, after telling his parents that he was being assailed by things he couldn't see or understand. He, along with the rest of the family, heard persistent footsteps upstairs when nobody was there. He begged his parents to move back to their previous house.

The ghostly footsteps were a bit of a mystery—even to Ernie. He said the footsteps seemingly walked right through closed doors, just as if they were wide open. Neighbors and friends scoffed and said the Dubreys had only heard noises made by the wind blowing down their old chimney. Ernie went to work and tore the chimney down, replacing it with a new one—not once, but twice. Still the footsteps and other odd sounds continued in the house.

One memorable night, Ernie remembers being awakened by a commotion in the boys' bedroom. His two sons slept in twin beds at the time. As he crept carefully into the room, Ernie saw that the boys were sound asleep. Something else made his jaw drop. There, standing next to one of the beds, was a tall man, dressed all in black. The man had no face. To say that Ernie was disconcerted would be a gross understatement. He began screaming loudly at the male figure in his sons' bedroom. Soon, his wife and children were all wide-awake. As soon as he hollered, the ghost simply evaporated, right before his eyes.

Soon after moving into the house, the Dubreys decided that they needed more insulation in the attic. Ernie climbed up there to get the project underway. Besides about six inches of dust, they found two interesting objects. One was an old sword. It was about three feet long and was inside a scabbard. When Ernie first pulled the sword from its dusty scabbard, he noticed spots on the blade. He thought they were probably rust, but his kids preferred to believe they were blood. Ernie went along with their fantasy, just to enhance the mystery.

As we spoke, Ernie tried to remember a name inscribed on the blade. It finally came to him: Augustus Ludwig. He was never able to trace the name or the origin of the sword, but surmised it was possibly presented to Ludwig in some kind of post-Civil War ceremony. Many Saranac residents fought in the war, but neither Ernie nor I was able to find any local reference to the name on the blade. There are Ludwigs in the area, but none lay claim to an ancestor named Augustus.

He eventually placed the sword over the fireplace mantle in his living room, and it rested peacefully in that spot for quite some time. However, the family contended that the sword was somehow bewitched, and I spoke to two visitors to the house who agreed. When they were sitting around one evening, they heard sounds as if the sword was jiggling. As they turned to look, it slowly rose from its hooks, floated out into the middle of the floor, and dropped with a loud "clang." Newcomers would be blown away, according to Ernie, but he and his family always laughed and simply told the ghost of Farmer John to "knock it off!"

I asked Ernie what eventually happened to the sword. He recalled that he sold it to a local woman dealing in antiques. She was well into her nineties when I tracked her down. What she told me was a complete surprise: she loved the sword, she said, and had begged Ernie to sell it to her, but he always refused. So goes the mystery.

There was something else in the attic. Next to the sword was a very old violin in its case. Ernie said the instrument was "in shambles." He felt compelled to have it repaired and brought it to a shop in nearby Plattsburgh to have the work done. The violin then found a home on his bedroom dresser.

While visiting Ernie one day, his Uncle Walter Brooks picked up the old violin and began to fiddle a tune. When he was finished, Ernie returned the violin to its case and set it on his bed. When he returned a bit later to put the violin back on his dresser, he was stunned to find the case open. He looked inside and found the violin again in shambles, just as it was when he discovered it in the attic. Not to be outdone by a ghost, Ernie carted the broken violin back to Plattsburgh and paid to have it restored once again.

Ernie's mother-in-law came to the house one day and asked if she could play a tune or two on the "spirited" instrument. She did so without incident. When her little recital was over, she put the violin back in its case, took it back upstairs, and placed it temporarily on Ernie's bed. One more time, when Ernie returned to his room, he found the violin in a shambles. This time Ernie said it was literally blown apart, as if by some unseen force. Ernie didn't give up or give in. He had it repaired one more time, replaced it on the dresser, and paid little attention to it for a long time.

Years later, his four grandchildren decided that they wanted to hold a séance in an effort to find out who the ghost or ghosts might be. Ernie said that by then they had nicknamed their resident spirit "John," perhaps after one of the previous owners, John Bruce or John Mahana (the owner before Mr. Bruce). They retrieved the violin from upstairs and placed it gently in its closed case on the kitchen counter. Candles were lit and all electric lights in the kitchen were doused. They sat around the table and began their incantations. Just as the séance got into full swing in the flickering candlelight, and the kids were fairly well mesmerized, Ernie decided to play a little trick. He lifted his knee and struck the table's middle leaf with a sound that put the fear of God into his young charges.

He didn't have long to gloat over his ruse. Moments later, they all heard "click, click." They turned toward the counter in time to see the clasps on the violin case flip up. The top was flung open, inflicting terror into every heart in the room. Never again did any-one ask to hold another séance in the old farmhouse on the Chazy Lake Road.

When the Dubreys moved into the house, an old panel door leading from the kitchen to the woodshed let in outside air during windy days. Ernie said that his rocking chair would often move back and forth with nobody sitting in it. He said at first he thought it was just the wind. Later, he wasn't quite so sure. A practical man, Ernie decided to replace the door with a solid, modern door with a push-button lock. The chair continued to rock on its own.

When I asked Ernie to try and remember what else might have been attributed to the ghost known as Farmer John, he sighed and asked if lights going on and off counted. I nodded and he continued. "We burned wood way back when," Ernie said. "Every two hours during the winter months, it was my job to get up during the night to stoke the two wood stoves we used to warm the house." Many times when he trudged down the stairs, he would find the kitchen lights turned on, despite the fact that he always turned them off before he went to bed. After the first dozen times, he didn't even bother to chew out his children. He knew it was the ghost of Farmer John.

Each night before retiring, Ernie would also flip on the yard light and lock that new kitchen door. Several times when he made those trips downstairs to load wood into the stoves, the new door would be wide open. Each time, he would check and find that the door's lock-button was pushed all the way in. Not to be outdone, Ernie started placing a kitchen chair backwards under the door-knob to wedge the door shut. That worked.

Ernie told me that he never got around to finishing one of the upstairs bedrooms. He was told that one of the previous owners raised chickens in that room. The doors had become warped and swollen over the years and had to be pushed very hard by an adult to close—and it would be impossible for a child to pry them open. Yet, more than once, he would climb the stairs at night and find the doors to that room opened wide.

Since Ernie Dubrey turned the house and property over to his son Douglas in 1986, the ghost of Farmer John has apparently decided to take a hiatus. Ernie says it was good riddance.

Bill Sackett Comes Back

Lu Sackett from Saranac, who was well into her eighties when I met her, became my good friend. Lu was an artist and a writer. I found her paintings to be at the same time bizarre and beautiful. She found my drawings to be the same. We got along famously. She's gone now, but my memories of her are poignant ones, as special to me today as they were back then. I have one of her delightful paintings in my home as a constant reminder of our many conversations.

I visited her home often just to relax and talk. Lu had seen and done a lot in her long and fruitful lifetime. Behind her on the wall was the photograph of a beautiful, young woman holding a cigarette delicately between the fingers of her right hand. She had been hired in the roaring twenties as a young teenager to pose for a cigarette company and got herself all "prettied up" for the photographer. Unfortunately, the advertising representatives forgot to bring along the brand of cigarettes she was hired to promote. Improvising, they found a competing brand and placed one of them in her hand in such as way as to hide the cigarette's name. It was a great story and still worthy of a chuckle in the telling many years later.

One of Lu's former husbands was named Bill Sackett. Like Lu, he was a most colorful character. Bill collected, bought, and sold antique bottles, among other things. He often rode around New York's North Country looking for more. Lu told me that her home had started its life as a one-room schoolhouse. Like many others that had served their purpose, this one was moved to its present location and turned into a home. Lu said that when she first spotted the house and property not far from the picturesque Saranac River, she fell in love with it, and she knew in her heart and soul that she would someday live there. Once she got inside to look it over, she didn't give her husband a chance to say no.

Soon after the young couple moved in, Lu says she began to hear the sounds of happy children both inside and outside. She sincerely believed that somehow the old walls had absorbed their laughter and revealed it to her from time to time many decades after.

Lu was blessed with many gifts. Among them was the ability to sense things about a building's past. If She and Bill saw an abandoned, dilapidated house while out bottle hunting, she would demand that he stop the car so she could approach the building and "feel" its history.

Peg Barcomb was among Lu's very closest friends. Peg is the one who first introduced Lu to me, starting a great connection that was shortened by Lu's untimely death a couple years later. Peg reminded me of a story Lu had related to me during one of our numerous chats. On one of the many occasions that she made Bill stop by an old house that had obviously not been occupied for a long time. Lu jumped from the car almost before it came to a complete stop, running up to the house and peering through the windows.

Although there were no furnishings inside, Lu could "see" a bed with a small pine box resting by its foot. She was instantly aware that the box had been constructed as a coffin for a little girl who had died in the house. Looking through the window of a shed attached at the rear of the house, she spotted a piece of white fabric. This was the cloth, she said, that had covered the little body. It had been placed in the shed during the remainder of the cold winter, awaiting a spring burial in the little box she had spotted by the foot of the bed.

Nowadays, if I heard such a story, I would attempt to do some research in an effort to verify Lu's story. It is impossible, though, at this late stage, as the location of the house isn't known. In any case, the tender tale of the dead child in the shed is certainly one to ponder.

Lu told me of a ride she once took with Bill to an open house at the old Keese homestead near Harkness, New York. The nearby village of Keeseville bears the family's name. Bill parked their car in front of the grand old home and went inside to see if they had any antiques for sale. Lu remained in the passenger's seat.

As she glanced around the spacious, tree-lined front yard. She was amazed to see a woman dressed in a costume that might have been worn in the nineteenth century. The woman wore a full-skirted dress and a bonnet, and she carried a fancy parasol in one hand. Lu wasn't surprised. She thought the present owner's wife had dressed up in a period costume to add the flavor of authenticity to the open house going on inside. She watched the woman for some time. It wasn't until Bill returned to the car that she realized there had been no such woman—at least not "in the flesh." Bill was convinced that somehow she was able to look through a magical window into the past from her seat in the car.

I was constantly mesmerized by Lu's stories, so much so that I often forgot to write them down. However, when Peg Barcomb and I were reminiscing after Lu's death, some of those conversations came back to me. It was almost as though Lu was whispering them in my ear. Peg added one of her own. During Lu's final year on this earth, Peg spent a great deal of time helping her to clean around the house. She also began, at Lu's request, to go through her possessions and make provisions for them.

During the cleaning process, Peg would take an object off a table or shelf, dust it thoroughly, and put it back. She kept a running inventory of every item in Lu's house. When she spotted something particularly intriguing, she would take it to Lu and listen to the memories it evoked.

Lu's husband Bill had died back in 1994. Some of the bottles he had collected were kept on a window shelf. Others were packed safely away in a back room. Lu got Peg's attention one day while they were working, and mentioned a bottle she spotted in the middle of a nearby coffee table. Peg was astounded. She had just finished cleaning the table and was certain there was nothing left on it, but there was no denying that there was something there now. Peg walked over to the table and picked up the bottle. Inside was a paper that had been rolled up and stuffed into the neck of the bottle. Peg said she pulled the paper out and was fascinated to find that it was an article she herself had written for a local newspaper years before.

Peg is a former historian in the area and had collected a number of old bottles connected with Rouses Point, where she lived at the time. She remembers that the writing on the bottle identified it as being from "Crook and Kane General Store." She and Lu scratched their heads. The only explanation they could come up with is that Bill came back just long enough to put the Rouses Point bottle where Lu and Peg would find it. And it wasn't just any old bottle. It was one Bill apparently wanted Peg to have, since she was the one who had done the research on it. That was a good day for Peg and for Lu.

Now that Lu is gone, Peg and I are guessing that Lu and Bill are taking bottle-hunting trips together, wherever they are. One has to wonder if she still makes him stop so she can look in windows. If so, we hope she spots us enjoying our reminiscences about her.

Leonard's Ghost

It took a while for me to convince Becky and Jim Leonard to sit on our living room couch in Morrisonville and tell of their experiences. My pen was flying. Becky owned and operated video stores in Clinton County. One of them was connected to their home in West Chazy. Another was converted from an old Morrisonville home barely fifty feet in front of my house. And yet another was a former auto repair shop.

I often warm up my guests with a few ghost stories of my own. It didn't take long when they visited our house for the juices to flow. Soon, Becky and Jim were both trying to talk at the same time. They had stories that my wife Kaye and I found wonderful and amazing.

Some time later, Kaye and I sat with the Leonards by the roadside during the Town of Schuyler Falls annual garage sale. During lulls in the action, I asked Becky more questions about her haunted house and shop in West Chazy. She and Jim moved into the old building at 7687 Route 22 in June of 1990. They purchased the property from Ron Marks, who owned and operated a hardware store in the front portion of the building. Becky planned to use that space for her first video store.

Becky was told that a schoolhouse was situated on the same spot as her home long ago. She later acquired an ancient photograph that confirmed the story. She heard that neighborhood hoodlums burned the school to the ground on the night before Halloween. "Cabbage Night," as that night is called in this area, was well known for its almost rampant vandalism. The shenanigans included the burning of haystacks, abandoned buildings, and overturned outhouses. Further proof of a previous fire was evident by virtue of the charred basement floor joists. Becky believes they left the floor supports intact after the fire and built the present structure on the old foundation. Neighbors also told her there could have been a church-related building on the site at one time in the distant past.

Becky recalls that her family had been living in the house for about two years before paranormal activity began. Their young son Nick was awakened often during the night and tearfully told his parents, "That guy came into my room again." Jim, who was a policeman at the time, decided to have a little chat with whatever spirit remained in the old building. He stood at the top of the cellar stairs where much of the odd activity had taken place and spoke in a loud voice: "Listen here. I don't mind sharing this place with you, if you're friendly. But, don't ever frighten our kids during the night. If you do, I'll bring a priest in here to exorcise the place and sweep it clean." Jim assured me that his children were never bothered again.

Becky says that she and Jim would often watch television two rooms down from what came to be known as "the ghost area." They would simultaneously catch a glimpse of movement out of the corner of their eyes, always close to a spare room located not far from their bedroom. A bathroom adjacent to the spare room was the site of strange sounds often described to Becky by her employees while tending to business out front in the video store.

There was a door connecting the apartment to the business. One interesting event convinced both Becky and Jim that they were never alone in the building. Becky says she was in her bedroom. Jim was in the spare room on the other side of the door and about five feet away from it. As each of them approached the door, the long handle began to turn on its own. It was as if someone was planning to open the door before they got there.

Becky spoke, asking Jim if he planned to come in. Jim spoke at the same time, asking Becky if she intended to come out. Neither had yet reached the door. They were frozen in place. For some time after, they each accused the other of playing a joke. The joke was on both of them.

The next day, as they were standing near the same door discussing the handle-turning incident, they were startled by a loud "BANG!" It came from the door itself, which shook so violently that the work schedules and other paperwork hanging on it swung back and forth for several seconds.

Jim, who is an all-around handyman, said he was doing some electrical work in the building. No matter how hard he looked, he couldn't find his circuit tester. In a last-ditch effort, he stood outside that spare room where much of the paranormal activity had taken place and spoke aloud once again to their resident ghost. "Listen," he pleaded. "I need that tester now if I'm ever going to get this job finished. I can't seem to find it. I need a little help here." At the moment, a basket on top of the roll-top desk next to him tumbled to the floor at his feet. Out of it fell the elusive circuit tester. If he wasn't a true believer before, he became one then.

He also confirmed Becky's story about seeing shadowy forms in the hallway. Each time he turned to look at them, they would disappear. The children were never bothered and were usually sound asleep in their beds at the time of the ghostly activity.

Then, there was the story of their lost camera. Becky was trying to take photos of some old movie posters to sell on the Internet. She had carried the camera with her up on a stepladder, taking shots of the posters on the floor. As she went to grab the camera one more time from the top of the ladder, it was gone. She and Jim searched the house. No camera. Frustrated, Jim did it again. He walked down the hall to that "special" spot near the spare room. He spoke to the ghost and explained how necessary it was to find the camera and finish the job. At that very moment, Becky hollered, "Here it is." He ran to the other room and she blurted out to him that the camera had suddenly materialized on the floor at her feet. They were both pleased and astounded at the same time.

Amidst the furious packing as they got ready to move from the old building in West Chazy to a much newer home in Cliff Haven on Lake Champlain, Jim says he strolled to the rear porch for a nostalgic last look around. He reflected on how much he had enjoyed living there but muttered aloud, "Except for that (expletive deleted) light out yonder that is always too bright on our house and yard." At that instant, the light on a neighbor's building went dark. He ran to tell Becky, but by the time they returned, the light was back on. Jim says he figured it was just their friendly ghost saying "So long. It's been good to know ya."

Jim and members of his family worked months to convert a century-old house in front of ours into another video store in the late 1990s. It was for them a major project. Jim and his dad often worked together, tearing out old plaster walls and erecting new ones. Jim and Jerry found some neat, old photographs and other interesting objects in the walls and on top of the beams. On more than one occasion, they could hear the sounds of children laughing and playing when no one else was around. It was eerie, but somehow comforting, to know that it had been a happy house at one time.

After the video store opened out front, I spoke to Becky and to several of the clerks who all said they had heard the sound of children's laughter. They also experienced strange sensations of "not being alone" while working late at night.

Some time later, Jim and his dad spent a lot of time renovating the second floor into a spacious rental apartment. One night, Jim came knocking at my front door. The hair on his arms and the on the back of his neck stood up straight as he explained what had happened to him a few moments before. He had been working on the apartment, pulling old paneling off the walls to reveal the fine, rounded corners of the original home's interior. As he exposed the old-fashioned plaster and lath, he had the almost overwhelming feeling that he was not alone in the room. Jim was a highly trained police detective, less than a year away from retirement at the time. His long experience investigating crimes had honed his sixth sense for feeling when things in a place or situation are not quite right. This was definitely one of those times. He instinctively backed up to the wall closest to the exit door and scanned the room very carefully. He said he couldn't see an actual form, but he knew that someone or something was there in the room with him. Jim did what Jim does best. He spoke to the "entity" aloud. "It's okay," he said. "I'm just making renovations so that another happy family can move in here. Please don't bother me and don't bother them when they arrive."

It's been several years since the apartment was finished and I know all those who have occupied it since that time. There have been no further problems with ghosts. The video store on the first floor has long since closed, but Jim uses it for storage related to another business and has no new stories about spirits.

As an addendum, I should add that when the Leonards moved their family to Cliff Haven, Jim invited the ghost from West Chazy to come along. One of these days, I'll bug him for an update.

St. John's Ghost

Through the years, there have been many stories of spirits haunting the area along the south side of Broad Street in Plattsburgh where St. John's Catholic School was located. It almost seemed like an afterthought when, in 2006, new reports began to come in about something very strange happening behind the school off Steltzer Road (formerly Riverside Road).

The first story came from college students from the area who decided to walk into the nearby Riverside Cemetery at midnight to see if they could detect any spirits. They had heard of strange photographs containing so-called "ghost orbs" that had been taken there in the past. Nothing out of the ordinary confronted them in the historic cemetery, but at the stroke of midnight, someone in the group chanced to glance across the road at movement he'd caught out of the corner of his eye.

A day care center had erected some playground apparatus behind St. John's School. It was an active, happy place during the day, used by laughing children at play. But not—normally—at midnight. On this night, though, a little girl could be plainly seen, swinging back and forth as if it were broad daylight. The college students were mesmerized by the sight and, for a time, couldn't speak. Soon the child disappeared. They compared notes as to what they had observed. They could only surmise that the child was a specter from another time. But who was she? Did she die there? Did she live in the area before the school was built? They scratched their heads and headed for their respective homes.

Two nights later, they met up with friends and began to tell their story. The friends were speechless at first—and with good reason. They, too, had decided to walk over to Riverside cemetery one night at midnight. They, too, happened to spot something across the street in the playground behind the school. And they, too, spotted a little girl swinging all by herself. Their story had an interesting variation. They actually left the cemetery and walked across the street and into the playground, keeping their eyes on the little girl as they went. She remained in sight until they approached within a few feet of her, and only then, faded from view. The two incidents happened independent of each other on different nights; and it was pure chance that their stories were shared.

St. John's school closed some years back, and the buildings were razed to make way for housing units. To this day, no one has a credible theory about the name of the little girl on the swings.

Minnie and Her Friends

I met my friend Amos Sorrell at St. Alexander's Cemetery in Morrisonville on the afternoon of November 7, 2006. Amos does work for the church and was digging a small grave for cremated remains. While he worked, Amos told me details of his "interesting" experiences in what is called "the old Minnie Boyea house" on the north side of Route 22B in Morrisonville, not far west of the Banker Road.

Amos has owned the wood frame house since shortly after Minnie died in the 1990s. He informed me that his grandfather did the original electrical wiring in the building. Before that, it had no inside running water or electricity. Amos spent a lot of time remodeling the interior of the old house so that a single mother and her children could move in. He told me that on several occasions, he felt a presence near him and could see a filmy figure in his peripheral vision. Each time he turned to see who or what was there, it would simply disappear.

He was never certain if it was his imagination playing tricks on him, but on one occasion, something happened that made him a true believer. He had been working feverishly to finish the remodeling job, as the family was getting impatient to move in. He said it was about two A.M. and he was on the second floor, pulling electrical wires through the walls to get that part of the job finished. Suddenly, he heard three very loud bangs. He said the walls shook, it was so loud. He knew instantly that the sound had come from somewhere downstairs. At first, Amos surmised that some of his friends had just closed a local bar on nearby River Street and were playing a prank on him. He went down the stairs very carefully and found nothing out of the ordinary—until he went into a pantry closet. Inside the pantry was a trap door leading down into the basement. The heavy door was set into the floor and had what is called a D-ring for lifting. Just a day or two before, a strong man who works for Amos had been unable to raise the trap door in the normal way. Frustrated, he grabbed a long, metal pole for leverage, placed it through the ring and tried with all his might to lever the door up and out of the floor. No luck. The trapdoor was stuck.

He and Amos concluded that it had been nailed shut many years previously. They decided to leave it that way, as there was an outside entrance to the cellar not far from the front of the house. Imagine his utter surprise when Amos opened the pantry door and saw that the trap door had not only been lifted off the floor, but was sitting crossways at an angle completely out of its recess. Amos said his first reaction was to flee the house on the run, but he caught himself and realized that he had a job to finish. He spoke aloud, saying, "I don't know who you are and what you want, but I would surely appreciate it if you could assist me in getting these electrical wires run." He finished his soliloquy and got back to the task at hand. The wiring was completed easily with no further interruptions.

He said that his tenant, Patti Todd, had also seen and felt something not human in the house while she lived there. Coincidentally, I had met with Patti only three days before, while I was selling raffle tickets for our church in the local mall. She stopped long enough for me to get at least part of her story. She said she lived in Minnie's old house between 1998 and 2001. While alone with her children, she would sometimes hear banging sounds "like hammering" toward the back of the house in what was formerly a wood shed. From her description, it seems that the noises were coming from the room now used as a pantry. Interesting.

When her son Adrian was twelve, he was awakened at night from a sound sleep to see a man standing in the doorway of his bedroom. The only description the frightened boy could give his mother was that the man was wearing suspenders.

Patti said she had a wall-mounted telephone in the kitchen. For no real reason, it would suddenly click on while she was across the room. After a while, she would talk out loud to the spirit in the house, asking him or her to cease and desist. Each time, the phone would instantly return to normal.

I asked Patti if there had ever been any odors associated with the ghosts in her house. She smiled knowingly and said that she often smelled delicious things cooking in the kitchen when she had nothing on the stove or in the oven. The odors were sometimes accompanied by distinct melodies from an invisible woman humming in the general area. At other times, she would get a whiff of Jean Naté perfume in parts of the house. She knew the smell, but had no Jean Naté perfume of her own at the time.

Patti also recalled an incident that occurred when her brother and his wife visited from California. The woman was awakened abruptly in the middle of the night by someone looking at her within inches of her face. She was so frightened that she could not offer any description of the ghostly intruder.

I feel certain that the female ghost is that of Minnie Bouyea. She and her sister used to sit behind my wife and me in church. Minnie was very strong-willed, and if she didn't like the homily, she often expressed her displeasure out loud. As for the ghost in suspenders or the one in the cellar—my, oh my—that's anybody's guess.

Surrounding Areas

Although my research largely focuses on Clinton County, I occasionally encounter leads to investigate in other areas. The stories that follow are too good to leave out of this volume.

The Potsdam Ghost

In communities all across the nation, old homes near college campuses have been converted into student apartments. This story has to do with one such house located at 115 Main Street in Potsdam, New York.

A friend with whom I worked asked if I would speak with her daughter who was attending Potsdam State at the time. It was December 2000. She said Trisha and her roommates had been having problems in the middle of the night. They were frightened more than once and believed the house was haunted. Even more important was their belief that the spirit or spirits there might be trying to burn the house down. That caught my attention.

I called Trish. She said they'd found a burner on their kitchen gas stove turned on at its highest setting, and that worried the young coeds. It had happened so many times that Trish was beginning to wonder if she might be losing her mind. After several of the stove burner incidents, the girls got together and compared notes. All swore an oath that they were not responsible. They would either come home late or wake up sensing something was amiss and find the burner turned on. They were all afraid, and they wanted to find an explanation.

I began to ask lots of questions. Trish's first-floor bedroom had a large, walk-in closet. Inside, against the back wall, was a small door that led nowhere. The closet's clothes rod was attached to the door. I was told that the other ghostly activities seemed to be focused on the main floor, mostly in the closet and the kitchen, which was adjacent to the bedroom.

I should interject here that at the time Trish and her friends were dealing with the stove burner events in Potsdam, another of my co-workers had a vivid dream in Plattsburgh, almost a hundred miles away. In the nightmare, the building housing Trish and her friends caught fire and was destroyed, and Trish was blamed for causing the blaze. The dreamer was afraid to tell anyone about the nightmare until I began to talk about the stove incidents weeks later. We compared dates and learned that at precisely the time of the dream, the burner was found turned on "high." Coincidence? Perhaps.

I continued my conversations with Trish. Her voice quavered as she told me that she had only lived in the old house for about three weeks when the stove burner incidents began to happen. She was certain that her friends would blame it all on her. She recalled the first "happening." She was alone in the house at nine o'clock one night. She sensed something wasn't right and walked into the kitchen. There she found that the right front stove burner had been turned on to its highest flame setting. Trish stood there looking at it, perplexed and bothered beyond words. Eventually, she shut it off and retired to her bedroom for the night. As she lay on her bed, unable to sleep, she tried desperately in her mind to find a logical explanation. Did she somehow brush up against the stove, turning the knob? No. That was impossible. It had a modern electronic ignition system. To light one of the burners, you would have to push the appropriate knob in, turn it until you heard the telltale "click, click" of the igniter, and then twist the knob further until the flame was lit.

By the time I spoke to Trisha, the same burner had been turned on at least four times. It was always on a weekend and always either Sunday night or early Monday morning. The latest such incident had happened only a short time prior to our first conversation. She said she got up to use the bathroom, looked out of her bedroom, and immediately saw that the stove was on again. But there was a difference. This time, it was the left front burner.

Things had begun to add up to something rather bizarre, and the sum total was scaring Trish half to death. She spoke again with her housemates, and she discovered that they all had seen or heard things they couldn't explain. There was an elusive spirit or spirits in their house.

One resident, Emily, was particularly distressed by the things that happened to her. She had lived in the other first floor bedroom since the year before. That was when she was awakened with the feeling that someone was in her room. She felt the presence as it sat on the foot of her bed. She quickly turned on the light and saw—nothing. Nothing, except the impression of a butt print remaining on the foot of her bed. She also often felt as though someone was talking near her. She could hear indistinct conversation, but no real words. Each time she turned to look, there was nothing out of the ordinary and the sound stopped.

A student named Molly also lived in that mysterious Potsdam house. She recalled being in Trish's room in November of 2000. They both heard someone walking down the stairs from the second floor. They saw the shadow of a small person as it turned the corner at the foot of the stairs. Emily said she heard and saw the same thing from her adjacent bedroom. One of them went out to see who had descended the stairs. No one was there. They went upstairs and checked with their friends. None had budged from their rooms.

Trish told me that others in the house often heard loud sounds that seemed to emanate from her bedroom. More specifically, they appeared to be coming from her walk-in closet with the strange door inside on the wall. The upstairs renters said it sounded like somebody was downstairs in that closet, pounding on the ceiling with a broomstick. Trish agreed. More than once, when both she and Molly were in her room, they could hear similar sounds, like someone pounding on the ceiling above the closet.

On another occasion when Molly and Trish were in Trish's bedroom, they were stunned to hear the anguished cries of a little girl. The child was screaming things like "No. Help me. Go away. Get off me!" The commotion was coming from Emily's room. They rushed in and found the bedroom a complete mess. Things had been knocked off the nightstand. The bed was in total disarray. Emily was curled up in a fetal position near the top of her bed. The child's voice was coming from Emily's mouth. She was pleading and crying for help.

They watched for a few moments, paralyzed by the spectacle. Finally, they decided that the only way to stop it was to try and shake Emily awake, as if from some horrible nightmare. They spoke softly, assuring Emily that she was all right, and gently shook her by the shoulders. Eventually, Emily awoke and returned to her old self. She was exhausted and had no recollection whatever of what had just happened to her.

In another incident, the boyfriend of another roommate, Meghan, began to moan in the middle of the night while sleeping there. She shook him until he came around; unlike Emily, he was petrified and completely aware of what had happened to him. He said he was awake at the time, but was paralyzed by something evil that came down on top of him, crushing the breath and life out of him. He couldn't move or speak. That's when his girlfriend heard the moaning. He said he was certain that he was going to die.

Trish discovered later that this happened at about the same time she first discovered the burner turned on in the kitchen downstairs. By now, all the girls were speaking freely, as if they needed to tell their stories to someone who would actually believe them.

The day I spoke to Trish, she was still shaking from an incident the night before. She and all of her friends in the house heard very loud, clattering noises in the kitchen, as if dishes were flying off the counter in every direction. None of the girls dared to investigate at that time, but the next morning they found their dishes all over the kitchen floor.

Her friend Meghan rented one of the second story rooms. She said her radio turned itself on at exactly two o'clock in the morning at least a dozen times. She added it never played music. Instead, it always switched onto the "tape" mode, with the accompanying light flashing in her eyes during the night. That was particularly odd to her, as Meghan never played tapes in the machine. Whenever she turned the unit on, it went directly to the CD mode.

I eventually learned that all the girls who lived there during the fall semester of 2000 had their own unexplainable experiences. Each agreed that she often felt someone watching her. Each had seen shadows out of the corners of her eyes. When they turned their heads to look, nothing was ever there.

I told Trish to try to get the little door in her closet opened. It had been nailed shut, but her boyfriend finally managed to swing the door outward. They found that whatever was behind it had been boarded up. They walked out back and saw that a former entrance door had also been blocked and several old wooden doors had been nailed over it from the outside. They spotted a small window higher on the house and climbed onto each other's shoulders to shine a light inside. They saw a small room with various objects still inside. Obviously, nobody had been in the room for many years. It had simply been closed off, both from the outside and from Trish's closet.

Why would an entire room be nailed shut and access totally removed? Unless...?

The renters decided to learn what they could of the building's history. They went to one of the owners and asked for details. They were told that a three- or four-year-old girl had died in the house long before she and her husband bought it. The tyke's wake had been held in the house, as was the custom in those days. The woman also told them that a priest had been brought in a few years before to bless the house or perform some sort of religious rites.

She told the girls further that student renters had reported ghostly happenings in the house at least twenty years before; they were the ones who had learned through old newspapers of the little girl's death there. The woman said many girls who rented rooms in the house had reported feeling someone there with them. A few even said they felt what seemed to be a little hand touching them, as if trying to get their attention.

That's when the landlords decided to bring in the priest. The priest himself said he also felt a presence there as soon as he stepped inside. Following his blessing, there were no appearances of the ghost for some years. That changed in 1999 when Emily felt someone come in and sit on her bed. From that point forward, the strange events became much more frequent.

These are the kinds of stories I would love to follow up on years later to see if the little girl returned or moved on to a higher plane.

Hodson Hall Hauntings

Noted lecturer and researcher into the world of the supernatural, John Zaffis, did a lecture and slide presentation about ghosts on the campus of North Country Community College in Saranac Lake on October 16, 2003. The noontime lecture was held in the David W. Petty Lecture Hall, located in the science building.

Later that afternoon, Zaffis consented to do a radio show in nearby Hodson Hall, which was built in the late nineteenth or early twentieth century to house the Saranac Lake General Hospital. Old photographs still kept at the college show the original building before hospital wings were added in later years. Hodson Hall was the first campus building renovated to house the college.

Many doctors and nurses who work long hours in a hospital setting will tell you their favorite, and sometimes not so favorite, stories of things that go bump in the night. Such stories abound in Plattsburgh, only about an hour away. Part of the old Champlain Valley Hospital is part of the present Plattsburgh State campus, while the old Physician's Hospital, constructed in the 1920s, is the core of the modern CVPH Medical Center across town. Dozens of doctors, nurses, and patients will tell you scary tales about those sites at the drop of a hat.

Now back to Saranac Lake. John Zaffis, outfitted with some kind of ghost detecting meter, accompanied North Country English Instructor Stacy Mascia and a student into the Hodson Hall basement. As they walked near a locked file storage area, adjacent to the original Saranac Lake Hospital's morgue, the meter began to go crazy, indicating that some kind of "presence" was there with them. They couldn't get the storage door open, and by the time a key was obtained, whatever it was had disappeared.

Stacy Mascia and the student were then allowed to take the meter themselves and investigate further. They walked slowly toward the Wilderness Recreation storage area across the hall and detected another presence (or perhaps the same one), much to their delight. As the instructor and her student carried the meter into the storage room, they both felt suddenly full, as though they had just put away a huge Thanksgiving dinner. Neither could explain it. At the same time, they said they could feel someone tugging at them. The sensations left them as they exited the room.

There are numerous stories connected with Hodson Hall, and those who tell them seem absolutely sincere in their belief that more than the living have been known to walk those old floors. One of these storytellers is my daughter-in-law, Sandy Baker, the college registrar. She has firsthand knowledge of otherworldly events in that building. Working alone late at night, she swears that she has heard footsteps outside her door, only to find that no one was there. She has checked the parking lot more than once and found no cars and no one else burning the midnight oil. Besides the footsteps, she has heard doors opening and closing for no earthly reason. It was unsettling each time, but not really threatening.

There's more. A lot more. At least twice in recent memory, members of the night cleaning crew insist they have seen the ghost of a woman dressed in white, engaged in the mundane task of washing windows on the second floor. As they approached, she simply vanished into thin air. To this date, apparently no one has been able to figure out who she might have been in life. Was it someone who worked there for a long time or who died there with the unfinished business of getting the windows squeaky-clean? Speculation among modern-day workers in the building appears to be that the window washer could have been an employee at the hospital in the days when tuberculosis sufferers flocked to Saranac Lake for the cure. It was imperative that all the rooms were kept spotlessly clean to prevent the spread of the dreaded disease. That explanation makes sense.

I leave you with this paraphrase of Shakespeare: "TB or not TB. That is the question."

Michael Is Cold

Carrie De Chavez is my granddaughter. She lives in Saranac Lake, New York, and is employed at a nearby Lake Placid nursing home known as the Uihlein Mercy Center. It is located only about a mile, as the crow flies, from the home and farm of Civil War era abolitionist John Brown. Readers will automatically associate him with the Underground Railroad, a network of sympathizers who created a conduit for slaves to make it from the southern states through New York and into Canada to find freedom.

More than once, the elder residents of Uihlein have reported to the staff that they encountered a young black boy in or near their rooms. Not only does he appear real, but he also converses with the patients. They say he is invariably crying, and when they ask him why, he tells them he is very cold. When they inquire as to his name, he always answers that his name is Michael. One woman said she felt so sorry for little Michael that she asked if he wanted to climb up onto her bed to be covered up with her warm quilt. Her motherly instinct had kicked in, and she begged him to come close so that she could wrap him in her blanket and cradle him in her arms. Every time she asked, he refused.

Area residents have said they believe there were hiding places in that vicinity where slaves were secreted inside underground rooms built for that specific purpose. There were said to have been reports that during one bone-cold North Country winter, the ground had collapsed onto a group of the slaves. At least some of them were believed to have perished in the mishap. Was Michael one of them? Who was Michael, anyway? So far, no one has positively identified him. Slave records were incomplete at best, and it is extremely difficult to find the names of those who used the Underground Railroad.

Carrie says she doesn't know if Michael is responsible, but she and others at Uihlein have stared in disbelief as water faucets in patients' bathrooms turn on and off, always when no one is in the bathroom. Either the patient or the worker first hears water running, then goes into the bathroom and watches incredulously as the faucets turn off without any human intervention.

Carrie says no one has ever really been frightened or threatened by Michael's presence, but they would all love to be able to bridge the gap between their dimension and his, so they could comfort him at last and perhaps help him to get warm.

The Ghostly Children
of Crown Point

My friend Calvin Castine and I have done hundreds of television documentaries in northern New York State. We've captured for posterity the images of many interesting people and places in a way that we think is rather unique.

Arto Monaco, designer, builder, and operator of the Land of Make Believe and dozens of other such theme parks around the country, was a wonderful subject. His ninety years on this earth were full and fruitful, and he was most unselfish in sharing his many creative talents with others in a million different ways. We visited him in his Upper Jay, New York, workshop and recorded at least nine, ninety-minute, uncut, uncensored, and completely unrehearsed interviews that are charming and wonderful, separately and collectively. We celebrated his ninetieth birthday by doing a show with him just six days before his death.

Back in October of 2002, as we chatted in his shop, I told Arto of my collection of true ghost stories. Arto had a story of his own for every occasion, and this was no exception. His tale this day, about some ghostly children in Crown Point, New York, was one I had not heard before.

Arto remembered an old federal-style house located fairly close to the famous Crown Point Bridge across Lake Champlain. It is in that general location that "Champy" or "Champ," the renowned Lake Champlain monster, has been seen by thousands of people for almost four hundred years.

In his travels far and wide, searching for animals to populate his Land of Make Believe theme park in Upper Jay, he was told that the woman who lived in that Crown Point home had some ponies for sale. Arto stopped by the house one day, introduced himself, and asked about the animals. The woman told him that he'd better make up his mind really fast, as she was about to move out. When quizzed as to her reasons, she snapped back that the blankety-blank place was haunted and she was completely fed up with the ghostly shenanigans she'd witnessed there.

The woman told Arto that a locked room to the rear of the top story of the house was said to contain the ghosts of several children who appeared from time to time dressed in Revolutionary War era clothes. She said that others who had peeked in had seen and heard the children laughing and playing in the room for many years. They described the spirits of the children as being fully formed, but transparent.

Because of her tremendous fear of the unknown, she had never ventured into the locked room to investigate. However, she was quick to point out that she had frequently heard their sounds from the hallway outside. Somehow, she worked up her courage one day and eventually decided to open the door after listening to the children from a safe distance. Slowly, she turned the key. Carefully, she grasped the knob with trembling fingers and cracked the door open just enough to peer inside. "There they were," she said, "laughing and playing just like normal kids."

Except for one thing—she could see right through every one of them.

Arto bought her ponies and found out soon thereafter that she had indeed sold the beautiful old home and moved away. Some time later, the house was severely damaged by fire. The fire chief reported that the blaze was "of unknown origin." The new owners had it completely rebuilt and restored using the original plans to its earlier splendor. There it sits today.

The story of the spirit children has become somewhat of a legend in the Crown Point area of Essex County, but no one seems to know who the original children were and why they were destined to play in that upstairs room for eternity. Were they kidnapped and killed in the initial war for our nation's freedom? Were the ghostly children responsible for the fire while playing upstairs? Perhaps it will be possible by some psychic means to contact their spirits and get the real story.

I don't know the answers. But there is one thing that I do know. Arto told me that after he purchased the ponies, the woman asked if he would like to go upstairs and have a look in the children's room. He said that he had respectfully declined her offer.

The Loyola Villa Ghost

Almost every time I meet someone new and we have a chance to converse for more than a few minutes, the subject comes around to ghost stories. I'm responsible for that. Over the years, I've collected some gems just by asking the question, "Have you ever seen a ghost or do you know about any haunted houses?" Whether they believe in ghosts or not, almost everyone has a story based either on their own experiences or those of someone they know.

My wife, Kaye, and I were invited to dinner with friends in September of 2001. Several of their family members were present. We talked about high school football, kids, home repairs, clocks, and antique accordions. We started to get mellow when our hostess, Millie Sears, began to serve her famous dessert called Apple Betty, topped with vanilla ice cream. Her daughter Lisa Bowlen was there, along with her husband, Neal. They drew closer to the table when I mentioned that I write true stories about ghosts in Northern New York.

Lisa's ears perked up and her eyes brightened. She pulled her chair very close to mine and soon we were off to the races. From 1991 to 1993, Lisa and Neal rented an apartment in a large building located on First Street in Port Kent, not far from the ferry that transports cars and people across Lake Champlain to and from Burlington, Vermont.

Lisa told me that the white and green wood-frame structure was known as Loyola Villa and had once been used as a Jesuit retreat. In more recent years, it had been turned into an apartment house with about a dozen rental units. The Bowlen apartment was on the first floor in the rear. Soon after moving in, they began to hear stories from other residents about strange goings on. However, they reserved judgment until unexplainable things began to happen to them.

Lights throughout their apartment began to flicker in spite of the fact that the entire electrical system was found to be faultless. Still, they were not totally convinced that they had a supernatural visitor—until one memorable night. Lisa said she set an empty soup can on the kitchen countertop. As she stared in wonder and disbelief, the can began to wiggle, and then assumed a life of its own. It started to bounce and wobble and "walk" across the width of the counter. It stopped dead on the very edge without falling off. To use Lisa's own words, "I freaked."

Lisa and Neal had friends who rented another apartment in Loyola Villa. It was also in the rear of the building. The Bowlens had electric heat, but their neighbors used a hot air furnace for warmth. Variously, both apartments would suddenly and inexplicably become very hot or very cold. Lisa said she would feel a blast of frigid air one moment, and the next moment it would be gone. Then the temperature would rise rapidly to the point where it would become almost unbearable. At no time could anyone, including technicians brought in to investigate, discover any sort of malfunction of the heating systems in either apartment.

They were perplexed, to say the least. But the temperature mystery paled by comparison with the events Lisa experienced one night. She and her husband were invited to visit with other guests in their friends' apartment. One of the guests made a derogatory racial slur in an attempt to be funny. Both Lisa and Neal found the situation most uncomfortable. Apparently, an unseen guest at the party also took issue with the man's comments. Perhaps it was the spirit of a Jesuit who had lived there in a bygone era. A beautiful, heavy, hand-blown glass butterfly was situated on top of the television set across the room. Everyone present watched agape as the butterfly slowly became airborne. It floated off the TV and picked up speed, shooting out into the room. It appeared to be directly aimed at the guest who had made the bad joke. Just before striking the stunned man in the face, it stopped abruptly and shattered in midair with an explosion of tiny glass shards.

Lisa said there was no mistaking the fact that an unhappy force had given all of them a lesson, especially the miscreant with the misguided racial comment. There is no record as to whether he changed his ways, but it's a good bet that the rest of the evening's conversation took on a completely different tone.

Lisa offered more recollections about Loyola Villa. She said she and Neal were sound asleep one night when she was jarred awake by an almost overwhelming sensation that someone or something was in the room staring at her. She sat up and peered into the darkness. Directly in her line of sight at the foot of her bed was the figure of a man. She said she could never forget what he looked like: he was scruffy, old, and not unlike what you might see in an old tintype photograph of a sea captain in the mid-1800s. She noticed also that the man was unshaven, with wild, grayish hair. He was clad in some kind of flannel shirt and very dirty pants. Lisa remembered being momentarily paralyzed with fear. Slowly, her unwelcome visitor reached out his hand as if to grasp her leg. She screamed a question: "Who are you?" There was no answer. Hearing the scream, Neal jumped up, but he failed to see the intruder, who simply faded from view after Lisa hollered.

After a time, the Bowlens moved from Port Kent and confessed that they were rather happy to be away from the Loyola Villa and its uninvited inhabitants.